EMPOWERING
HUMAN RESOURCES
IN THE
MERGER AND ACQUISITION PROCESS

EMPOWERING HUMAN RESOURCES IN THE MERGER AND ACQUISITION PROCESS

GUIDANCE FOR HR PROFESSIONALS IN THE KEY AREAS OF M&A PLANNING AND INTEGRATION

MARK N. CLEMENTE

DAVID S. GREENSPAN

CLEMENTE, GREENSPAN & CO., INC.

Management Advisors

Glen Rock, New Jersey

All inquiries should be addressed to:
Clemente, Greenspan & Co., Inc.
233 Rock Road, Suite 260,
Glen Rock, New Jersey 07452;
(201) 444-1236;
www.CGadvisors.com

ISBN 0-9671204-0-3

Clemente, Greenspan & Co., Inc.

Clemente, Greenspan & Co., Inc. is an M&A consulting and training firm that specializes in helping companies ensure the success of strategic mergers and acquisitions in order to increase shareholder value.

CG&Co. is comprised of veteran consultants with expertise in M&A planning and integration – as well as in strategic marketing, training and development, and organizational communications.

CG&Co. focuses on the synergy between the merger partners' people, products and processes to develop strategies and tactics that drive long-term corporate growth.

Mark N. Clemente and David S. Greenspan, SPHR, the firm's principals, are frequent speakers before major companies and business groups on the topics of pre-merger planning and post-merger integration, and are the authors of *Winning at Mergers and Acquisitions* (John Wiley & Sons, 1998).

CONTENTS

Section One

Empowering Human Resources in the Merger and Acquisition Process

Successful Mergers and Acquisitions
Require Broad Involvement of Human Resources   Page   1

HR's Role in Acquisition Planning and
Implementation: 10 Critical Success Factors   Page   11

Section Two

Role of Human Resources in the M&A Process Today: Results of a National Survey

How the Findings are Reported   Page   21

Timing, Volume and Nature of
Respondent Companies' Acquisitions   Page   27

Evaluating Managerial Performance of
Acquisition Planning and Integration   Page   35

Critical Post-Merger Issues   Page   47

HR's Current Role in
Acquisition Planning and Integration   Page   64

Post-Merger Integration: Tactical Execution   Page   77

Importance of HR in the M&A Process:
A Self-Assessment   Page   89

Future Role of HR in
Acquisition Planning and Integration   Page   101

Section Three

M&A Skills Development for Human Resource Professionals

Introduction   Page   115

Acquisition Process   Page   117

Due Diligence   Page   121

HR Due Diligence Checklist   Page   127

Employee Communications   Page   129

Communication Critical Success Factors   Page   134

Organizational Behavior   Page   135

Employee Sensing and Research   Page   140

Assessment and Selection   Page   146

Training and Development   Page   150

Marketing and Sales   Page   154

Conclusion   Page   157

Successful Mergers and Acquisitions Require Broader Involvement of Human Resources

*M*ergers and acquisitions (M&A) continue as a primary means of effecting speedy and substantive corporate growth, yet several studies indicate that more than half of all M&A deals fail to meet management's strategic, operational and financial objectives. Going forward, acquirers must ensure that their transaction does not become another corporate combination casualty.

There are literally hundreds of reasons why the M&A failure rate is so high. But many can be traced to the exclusion of human resource professionals in the pre-deal planning phase and the function's last-minute inclusion after the transaction has closed. It's a classic case of "too little, too late."

To help improve the odds of orchestrating a successful transaction, HR must be broadly involved in all phases of M&A – pre-deal planning, target company evaluations, due diligence, and post-merger integration.

What are the specific activities HR professionals should undertake to help ensure the success of their companies' M&A program? It depends on the various, and inter-related, stages of the M&A process.

M&A Planning and Due Diligence – Where's HR?

The traditional focus of M&A has been on "making the numbers work." Typically, an investment banker or corporate development officer presents an acquisition candidate to management. If doing the deal makes financial sense, the wheels are set in motion and the due diligence phase begins.

Due diligence keys primarily on financial, legal and regulatory, and accounting and tax issues. Thus, when everything in the examination checks out, the merger partners plunge forward – *assuming* that the strategic benefits of the merger will necessarily fall into line. Statistics on the failure rate of M&A transactions suggest this is erroneous thinking.

The financial and legal aspects of M&A planning are critically important to the success of any transaction. But the traditional "ledgers and liability" orientation toward M&A planning highlights its principal shortcoming. If people issues are so important to the success of the deal, how can such little focus be paid to those issues in the strategy development, target company screening and due diligence phases?

Clearly, in most cases, the merger partners have not sufficiently assessed the strategic variables that lie at the heart of the deal; these include the all-important "people component." When a strategic vision drives an acquisition – as opposed to cost-cutting synergies or stock prices – it requires the critical up-front participation of HR professionals to assess the valued human assets that never show up on a balance sheet or income statement. What's more, identifying key human assets in a target company and quickly taking steps to keep them from walking out the door on announcement of the deal is an HR-related imperative every company must take. Yet, historically, HR comes into the M&A process too late to make this vital contribution.

In most companies, HR gets involved in the M&A process well after the initial pre-deal planning. Once the up-front groundwork has been laid and the deal announced, the legal, financial and accounting participants have all moved on to the next deal or gone back to work. HR is left with the hard part: developing communications strategies; aligning payroll, benefits and compensation paradigms; and trying to meld disparate processes and corporate cultures.

Unfortunately, by this point, key employees have headed for the exits. Those remaining are mired in confusion and inertia, and HR is forced to play catch up. Is there any wonder why after the first six months, most merged firms are left with less value than on the day the deal was announced?

HR: The Power to Make the Deal Succeed

HR professionals must participate at a higher level and play a much broader role in the following areas:

Acquisition Strategy

HR professionals should be among the senior managers who help guide the strategic vision of an M&A transaction. Unless it's a pure asset acquisition (e.g., obtaining manufacturing facilities or sources of raw materials), every deal involves securing people – people who possess distinct skills and capabilities. Those attributes will be needed to advance the merged company's strategic objectives.

But HR professionals must familiarize themselves with their company's business, strategic and marketing plans. This will put them in touch with the business issues that drive M&A decision-making. It is from this vantage point that people issues can best be linked to the very business strategies that spawned the acquisition in the first place.

Target Company Screening

Once merger or acquisition candidates have been determined, HR can play a valuable role in screening and evaluating those companies. Contributing a *people* perspective to a process that is traditionally focused on numbers will reduce the likelihood of the acquiring company making a disastrous decision on a would-be merger mate.

Many corporate marriages, much like those between people, have an underlying element of incompatibility that dooms them from the start. HR professionals can contribute to the evaluation process by assessing such crucial variables as a work force's possible response to an acquisition, marketplace perceptions of the employee base, and organizational differences that may exist in the merging companies' collective belief systems and attitudes. Culture is one important part of the investigation. But there are many others factors that determine the level of "integrate-ability" of two companies. HR professionals are clearly the best judges of these distinctly people-oriented issues.

HR Due Diligence

As mentioned, in traditional due diligence, HR issues are not typically addressed with the same level of scrutiny as financial, legal and tax considerations. Including HR as early as possible in the process makes the entire due diligence effort a more comprehensive and informed undertaking.

Issues brought to light via *HR due diligence* will help shape the longer term integration effort and help guide the scope and pace of the non-HR aspects of the acquisition effort. Following are the key areas of investigation:

> **Culture**
> The broadest issue confronting the HR professional is

corporate culture. Ideally, HR will have identified the basic cultural issues during the target-screening phase. However, if this is HR's first involvement in the evolving transaction, an overall cultural analysis must be performed. What is the organizational structure of the target organization? What are the overriding perceptions and assumptions that drive managerial decisions and behaviors within the company? How are employees hired, evaluated, promoted, terminated? How are employees motivated and compensated? The answers to these questions will impact the performance of both the acquired and acquiring companies' work forces — and, ultimately, the bottom line of the merged firm.

➤ **Employee Composition**
Following the cultural assessment should be a detailed analysis of the target company's employee base. Data on such variables as the number of employees and their demographic and socio-economic composition must be collected. The results of this analysis should be weighed against your initial cultural assessment to guide the process of devising integration, communication, and change-management initiatives. For example, if the work force is older and more formal than that of your company, the communications content and media would likely be different from those employed to reach a young and informal work force. A more conservative employee base would also dictate the design of particular organizational change strategies.

➤ **Key Employees**
As the analysis narrows, HR can help to pinpoint the key contributors to the target's intellectual asset base. Of utmost importance is quickly devising ways to safeguard those assets. As we all know, people are where the true value lies within any company. But HR must determine who the target company's *key* employees are. And, of these, which are viewed as *must keep* and which as *likely to lose?* In the event that yours is a product- or market-driven transaction (as most deals are

today), HR can work with the marketing due diligence team to identify the individuals who will head up specific product categories or departments – those which will be particularly critical in the merged company. These and other key managers must be targeted early and contacted *upon announcement of the deal* so that retention strategies can be immediately enacted. Think with a defensive mindset. Remember: the first thing an acquired employee does the day of the announcement is identify his or her options. Calls to newly acquired key employees from headhunters and competitors are more the rule than the exception. It is the HR professional's responsibility to alert management to these potential losses of value and to devise speedy retention strategies. Designing attractive benefits and compensation packages is one way to ensure employee commitment and retention post-merger. Clearly, this is HR's area of expertise.

➤ **Compensation**

The compensation structure of the target company must be quickly assessed and compared to that of the acquirer. Salaries, bonuses, commissions, severance agreements, SERPS and ESOPs must be identified not only for valuation purposes, but also for critical integration activities. If the acquisition goes through, unequal compensation levels will more than likely be issues of contention among the new co-workers. This factor can undermine any retention programs underway. Also, HR's identification of severance packages and whether they are more attractive than current salaries can help management identify the key players who will likely be gone when the dust settles. Creating an environment of fairness and equality will go a long way towards boosting morale and driving a successful integration.

➤ **Benefits**

Separate and distinct from compensation issues are the current benefits of the target. HR must perform a detailed analysis on the target's pension, 401(k), health and welfare plans to identify any potential incompatibilities, as well as liabilities and unreported assets. This is an exhaustive undertaking, and the results will greatly impact the valuation of the target. Issues such as whether the pension plan is adequately or under-funded could affect the ultimate purchase price of the transaction. And often, after reviewing collective bargaining agreements, multi-employer plans, SERPs and post-retirement plans, major liabilities will be unearthed – again, impacting the final price of the deal. Information collected on the target's health plans will lay the groundwork for a conversion to the merged firm's health plans after closing. Issues such as vendor selection, actuarial and benefits consultants, and degree of coverage can be addressed post-merger. But, often-forgotten critical sticking points such as COBRA can impact the negotiations before the deal is even announced because of the potential for acquired employees to elect coverage while waiting for the deal to close. Many critical health and retirement liabilities will go unchecked unless HR plays a pivotal role in this aspect of the due diligence process.

Integration Planning, Communication and Training

Setting the stage for post-merger integration is arguably the most arduous and essential aspect of HR's role in the acquisition process. This step lays the groundwork for an expeditious timetable that includes measures to retain valuable employees, maintain and accelerate operations, and boost revenues. The primary roles of HR during this phase are developing strategies for retaining and protecting the acquired human capital and planning the alignment of benefits, compensation, and health and welfare processes. Once these are established, HR can then focus on strategic staffing – the most significant determinant in cultivating the merged firm's requisite skill base.

The M&A graveyard is lined with the carcasses of companies who allowed cost-cutting to undermine a skills-based approach to staffing. Unfortunately, management often makes post-merger staffing decisions prematurely by putting people in place without systematically determining the roles they will play in the merged firm. Valuable people – those who can make a contribution to the merged firm or who would be central to the integration process – are lost because management makes cost-reduction-oriented staffing decisions without growth-focused forethought.

A determination must be made regarding the skills and competencies needed to support the merged company's growth initiatives. And only by tapping the expertise of HR can an acquirer mine the full range of skills and capabilities resident in the target company. Consequently, HR must take the lead in the assessment and selection process on which key managerial staffing decisions will be based.

Upon closing, detailed communication and training initiatives must immediately be set in motion. Sadly, most companies begin to address these issues too long after closing. Valuable employees walk out the door while HR is forced to slap together communication strategies that – if rolled out earlier – would have prevented defections to your competitors. The primary goals of post-merger communications should be to inform, and, more importantly, to inspire! Communications must convey compelling reasons why the merged firm is now a better place to work. Communications must achieve buy-in and, in doing so, build strong commitment to the merged firm's strategic vision. Only HR truly has its finger on the pulse of the acquired employees. Only HR can shape the organizational mindset that will move the merged firm forward in the marketplace. Therefore, HR must take a leadership role in these most important areas.

From a training standpoint, acquired employees must be trained in the customs, habits and history of their acquirer. An informed acquired workforce is a stronger, more productive and more loyal one. Quickly sharing knowledge with your acquired employees will boost morale and establish the bonds necessary to effect true teamwork. An environment that demonstrates a commitment to training, development and career pathing will serve this mission.

While all these steps can help broaden HR professionals' perspectives and heighten the contributions they make to their firms' acquisition programs, many HR specialists do not have the requisite knowledge of the extremely multi-faceted and complex M&A process.

The Clemente, Greenspan & Co. national survey, which is detailed in Part Two, found that the vast majority of HR professionals feel they lack the background and technical training to broadly contribute to their companies' M&A efforts. Training is clearly needed. For HR professionals to be more involved, they must be educated in each of the various phases of the M&A process. In the heat of a transaction, HR must readily understand how companies make acquisitions, how they review candidates, and how they map out the tactics necessary to effect corporate growth through corporate combinations.

HR professionals can and should play a greater role in M&A. But those who have not yet gained the requisite experience must prepare themselves.

In today's market and in the years ahead, there is a distinct possibility that — at any moment — HR professionals at all levels will be called upon to help ensure the success of their companies' acquisition initiatives.

The stakes are high for HR. So too are the rewards.

NOTES

HR's Role in M&A Planning and Implementation:

10 Critical Success Factors

*T*here are many reasons why the input of human resource professionals is necessary to ensure successful M&A transactions.

Following are actual case studies illustrating 10 critical success factors that tie directly to HR issues (general management, compensation, benefits, staffing, communications, and training and development) in pre-deal planning and post-deal integration. Awareness of these factors will help to empower HR professionals in all phases of their companies' M&A program.

1. Address HR issues in acquisition strategy development

Two major electronics firms were vying for a highly sought Internet company to gain a presence in that burgeoning market. One firm involved HR in its acquisition strategy development process. The other did not. The HR professionals who were involved brought to management's attention an industry norm – the importance of stock-based compensation to Internet company employees. The company that involved HR in the initial phase of its M&A planning structured its offer as a stock-based transaction. It also built in equity incentives as an employee retention strategy for the target firm's senior managers. Consequently, it was this company that won out over the rival bidder – which had failed to recognize this key compensation issue that directly impacted its acquisition strategy. After closing, new employees were excited to be part of an organization that had looked out for their collective futures.

2. Involve HR in target company examinations

A major industrial products company sought an acquisition to strengthen its presence in a given regional market. The would-be acquirer narrowed its search down to two target companies. Central to its acquisition goals was gaining a strong, deeply entrenched sales force – and each target seemed to offer one. Indeed, the sales force was the key asset to be acquired. The acquirer assigned its HR director to conduct personnel-related research *prior to* making contact with either of the target firms. The findings of this research were critical. One of the target firms had been experiencing unusually high turnover in its sales force – a situation that might very well be exacerbated in the wake of the transaction. Consequently, the acquirer opted to make its acquisition solicitation to the firm with the more stable sales force. The acquisition was effected successfully and post-deal employee retention was high.

3. Factor in key HR issues in the preparation of pre-deal contracts

A publishing company failed to involve HR in the process of drafting its "offer letter." The solicitation was made. And once the due diligence process commenced, HR needed to review the target's personnel policies and procedures and conduct evaluations of key personnel. The deadline for completing the deal was looming. And the structure of the negotiations had clearly omitted the right for the acquirer to gain the necessary access to records and people. This created a situation in which the HR due diligence team was unable to conduct its evaluations in timely fashion. Had the access and timetable issues been addressed in the pre-deal contract, HR would not have run into the highly problematic roadblocks that it did. Instead, HR was forced to perform compressed reviews of the acquired workforce *after closing,* which led to an extended period of confusion among both the acquired and acquiring employees, and an extraordinarily high level of employee turnover. Productivity immediately declined and HR was forced to play catch-up in the areas of morale, retention, and motivation. Whatever synergies might have been expected by management were gone.

4. Ensure that HR due diligence focuses on issues of cultural compatibility and incompatibility

Evaluating a target company's cultural characteristics is central to HR due diligence. In the case of a major consulting firm acquiring a smaller competitor, the acquiring firm failed to assess the seller's entrepreneurial management approach. This differed drastically from its own consensus-driven, decision-by-committee procedures. The deal went through. However, soon after closing, tremendous in-fighting resulted from the stark contrast in managerial methods. The acquired employees were confused and distraught over the delays in managerial decision-making; the acquiring company's managers were unnerved by the new employees' free-form ways of doing business. Initial attempts at aligning practice areas were severely stalled and widespread employee defections resulted. Word of the internal confusion quickly spread to the marketplace. Key prospects about to hire the consulting firm backed away from their commitments and pursued relationships with more stable firms. Many clients, unsure of continuing their relationships with the consulting firm for other reasons, found this a convenient excuse to retain other companies. A six-month period of lost business and strained customer relations followed, leading to a long-term downturn in business while the rest of the industry thrived. Had HR had the opportunity to assess these profound incompatibilities in management styles, two options could have been pursued: development of a management orientation program with clear guidelines, or walking away from the deal to find a more compatible partner. Instead, this company experienced a 40% attrition of the acquired company's employees in six months and irreparable damage to its brand name.

5. Ensure HR takes the lead in integration planning

A diversified holding company embarked on an aggressive acquisition program for its five main lines of business. Corporate management charged the operations managers of each unit with overall acquisition planning – including integration program design and implementation. Input from the corporate HR department was never offered, nor solicited by the operations people. A total of 20 acquisitions were conducted over a one-year period. In more than half of those transactions, employee defections far exceeded the typical 15%-25% of employees who leave in the wake of an acquisition. (In some cases, the employee defection rate soared above 50%.) In the second year of the acquisition program, corporate HR was asked to take a lead role in integration planning. Its first step was to determine the common practices in each operating unit that had been successful. It then performed an analysis of the best practices that would translate across all company lines. Ultimately, HR detailed those best practices in a process manual that was distributed to all operating heads. In the company's next few acquisitions, productivity increased and employee defections decreased significantly.

6. Avoid making hasty decisions on personnel cutbacks

Upon the close of its multimillion-dollar acquisition, a major insurance company moved quickly to cut back on personnel. Management immediately fired the acquired firm's entire accounting department. But shortly after handing out the pink slips, management realized that the only people who could successfully meld the accounting and payroll systems of the combining firms were the same people who were cut loose. Management was forced to try to rehire the fired workers, but many had landed other positions. The company was able to rehire only a few. (Most said they would rejoin the company only as high-paid independent contractors, who collectively would be paid more than what their original salaries totaled.) In this case, people were cut hastily – well before the operational and administrative requirements of the merged firm were identified. The result was devastating. Employees (some who had worked for their company for over 20 years) found that the first paycheck they were to receive from their new employer was not ready on payday. Employees using direct-deposit were forced to re-establish their accounts at their bank in person. And, even worse, accounting was now being staffed by fired employees who infused negative sentiment into the workplace on a daily basis. Members of the accounting department who had been with the acquirer began to resent working alongside those being paid twice as much as them. The double impact of compensation inequity and bad blood soon spread to other back office departments. Morale has still not recovered and defections from the acquirer continue to be high.

7. Conduct employee sensing throughout all phases of the integration process

The acquisition of a chain of retail stores by a larger competitor was proceeding smoothly in the months following the transaction's close. Both managerial appointments and the alignment of administrative functions were effected swiftly. Management had gauged the sentiments of the acquired employees and tailored employee communications to assuage their initial fears and concerns. Unfortunately, several months later there was increasing discontent among the acquired company's employees (the result of failed attempts to create joint teams in the launch of several major strategic initiatives). Management had stopped "taking the pulse" of the acquired company's workforce and, thus, failed to spot the swelling discontent. Initial employee research had been conducted. But management failed to do subsequent employee sensing to monitor shifting sentiments, which were undermining ongoing integration efforts. This company made a common mistake – it did not realize that communication needs to be two-way. Many merged companies send out a constant barrage of memos, emails and other missives to the combined workforce in hopes that this will suffice as merger communications. But they make little or no effort to gauge the audience's response to those communications. This is necessary to monitor the success of ongoing communication initiatives and to take corrective actions, where necessary.

8. Design training and development programs to directly support the merged company's strategic objectives

Cross-selling was at the heart of a merger of a commercial bank and an investment company, whose goal was to market a full array of insurance, brokerage, credit card and banking products to customers of the combined firm. But understanding and selling consumer banking products is vastly different from selling securities, mutual funds and insurance policies. Bankers, investment advisors, and insurance salesmen are not interchangeable. Initial efforts to generate revenues through cross-selling failed miserably. Why? Because management failed to recognize that the combined sales force had to be formally trained to sell the new line of products and services – offerings that they had never sold before. The backlash was very tangible. Customers once comfortable buying particular services from the bank were met with hard-sell tactics and salespeople they had never met. Within weeks of the transaction's close, 15% of the customer base took their most profitable business across the street to a "less complex" institution where they could resume a more personal relationship. Had HR professionals been involved in the strategic development of the acquisition, they could have worked with sales to quickly develop a focused training program that would have leveraged the combined company's strongest relationships instead of alienating its key customers.

9. Take a disciplined approach to assessment and selection of key managers

In most cases the dominant company in a "merger of equals" dictates which managers will receive the top positions in the combined firm. That does not mean that that company necessarily has the people deserving of those positions. In a combination of two healthcare companies, the more dominant merger partner assigned its top people to the top spots. In actuality, those people's counterparts from the acquired firm — by and large — had the better credentials, experience and managerial potential. (And it was those more talented managers who quickly left after the major executive appointments were announced.) Politics, obviously, drive many senior-level personnel appointments made post-merger. But the most objective acquirers seek the assistance of their HR professionals to systematically determine which managers have the requisite skills ... regardless of which organization they came from.

10. Implement ongoing employee communications to support integration

Employee communications should not stop after the initial post-deal announcements. Rather, they are necessary to support all phases of the integration process. Consider the case of an East Coast consumer products company that acquired a competitor based in the Southwest. Only very basic information on the acquisition was provided to employees upon close of the deal. However, the geographic distance between organizations necessitated detailed communications of an administrative, operational and strategic nature to meld the disparate operations. Management's failure to conduct ongoing communications hampered attempts at integration. The dearth of communications also kept the merger partners from quickly aligning their products and selling strategies — thus preventing them from realizing the early market-share gains they sought. Conversely, early market share losses continued well into the third quarter after the acquisition. The disappointment spread from management to Wall Street analysts, who began to downgrade the investment rating of the company's stock. Its share price swooned while the rest of the market moved strongly higher. Many key executives saw their stock options become worthless and began to defect to competitors that offered attractive sign-on bonuses. Had it been involved by senior management, HR could have orchestrated a comprehensive communication program that extended beyond the closing date. Most of the company's problems could have been averted.

More than ever before, senior management is recognizing the essential role of human resource professionals in the M&A process. But where do companies stand in terms of the specific responsibilities they currently assign to HR? And what do HR professionals, themselves, feel they should be contributing to the complex M&A process?

A national survey was conducted to find out. The results follow.

The Role of HR in the Merger and Acquisition Process:

Results of a National Survey

*A*ttending to the critical "people issues" that pervade mergers and acquisitions (M&A) – and which are central to the success of M&A transactions – has necessitated increasingly broader involvement of human resource professionals in all aspects of M&A planning and integration.

Indeed, the role of HR has been steadily expanding in recent years. The reason: corporate management has sought to reverse the tremendous failure rate of M&A transactions by focusing more acutely on the identification, retention, and cultivation of human assets involved in any strategically driven corporate combination.

It is widely held that HR must be involved broadly in mergers and acquisitions. *But little has been documented on the specific activities HR coordinates in the overall merger and acquisition process.* For this reason, Clemente, Greenspan & Co. undertook a national research study in which:

➢ A print questionnaire was sent to 3,500 companies with more than 2,000 employees The individual who serves as the company's senior HR executive was asked to respond. Respondents were asked detailed profiling questions to determine their eligibility such as their name, title, primary area of responsibility, and size of HR department. In order to elicit the highest level of candidness, respondents were assured that their identities and company names would not be printed in this report.

➤ Four-hundred and thirteen (413) surveys were returned via a fax-back response mechanism – and a series of one-on-one personal interviews were conducted

➤ Respondents were queried on the current role they play in M&A planning and integration; what role they *feel* HR should play in the M&A process; and what M&A-related training they view as being beneficial to heighten HR's contribution to ensuring the success of corporate mergers and acquisitions.

Clemente, Greenspan & Co. plans to conduct this study annually to monitor the changing role of HR in the merger and acquisition process.

It is the firm's hope that we will witness a progressively substantive contribution being made by HR. Increasing the odds of success in the complex merger and acquisition process depends on it.

How the Findings are Reported

Respondents were asked to indicate their involvement in acquisition-related activities and to assess their companies' past M&A efforts. A series of questions sought to solicit attitudinal information relative to the respondents' desired role in acquisition planning and integration.

Questions relating to respondents' attitudes were structured as scale items. Other queries asked respondents to check one or more boxes to indicate the M&A activities in which they have been involved.

The survey data are reported as follows:

➤ The findings of all scale questions are reported as an average ranking (on the scale of 1 to 5) and, in many cases, by the percentage of respondents citing each rank number

➤ The findings of non-attitudinal questions are reported solely as percentages

➤ Observations are provided for each question. These subjective assessments are based on the statistical data, the one-on-one interviews that were conducted with selected respondents – as well as insights gained from Clemente, Greenspan & Co. merger and acquisition consulting engagements, many of which involve direct interaction with human resource professionals.

Primary Area of Responsibility

Issue

This survey targeted senior HR professionals – those with the title of Vice President or Director of Human Resources. Since each company has its own unique structure, and the human resource function within each organization operates differently, it was important to determine the respondent's primary area of oversight or management. To ensure that those surveyed were in the most senior management position, respondents were asked to indicate their primary area of responsibility.

Findings

The initial profiling tool used in the survey helped to ensure the desired composition of respondents. An overwhelming 86% of respondents stated their primary area of responsibility as human resource management. The remaining 14% of HR management surveyed were responsible for benefits (5%), compensation (4%), and for organizational development (3%). One percent (1%) of the respondents cited training and staffing as their primary areas of responsibility.

"Acquisitions pose one of the greatest challenges to HR management today."

Director, Employee Relations
Medical products manufacturer

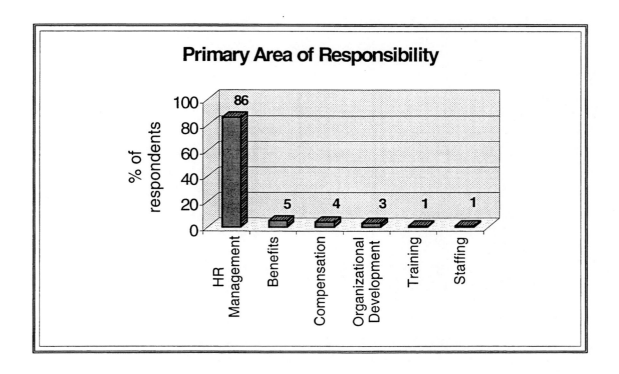

Primary Area of Responsibility

Observations

With 86% of the respondents citing overall "human resource management" as their primary area of responsibility, it is clear that the study generated substantive input from senior HR executives in the universe of companies surveyed.

Issue

M&A is impacting virtually every industry sector. In certain industries the growth is being sparked by deregulation; in others, competitive forces; and in others the driver is changing market conditions. This study, being national in scope, encompassed more than 100 Standard Industrial Classification codes which were then categorized into 12 basic industry segments.

Findings

Of the 413 companies responding, the most responses came from industrial product manufacturers (14%). The next four most common industries responding were high technology (13%), healthcare/medical (12%), consumer product manufacturers (11%) and financial services (9%). The remaining responses came from the following industry sectors: chemicals and pharmaceuticals; energy; and retail and distribution with 7% each; and business services; engineering/construction/real estate; hospitality and leisure; and media and communications each with a 5% weighting.

> *"The key asset in any acquisition is people. How can HR help but be a key player?"*
>
> **Senior VP, Human Resources**
> **Retail supermarket chain**

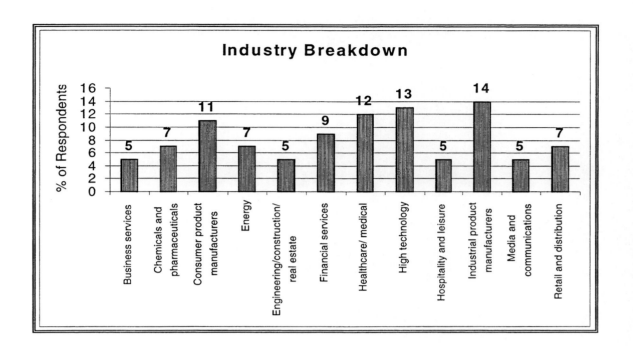

Industry Breakdown

Observations

Twelve distinct industry groupings provided feedback on their companies' M&A activities making this survey the broadest endeavor of its kind. Fifty percent (50%) of the 413 responses came from four industry groups: consumer products manufacturers (11%), health care/medical (12%), high technology (13%) and industrial manufacturers (14%). There was balanced input from manufacturing, product and service companies rounding out a vast sample from HR directors in virtually every type of business. The responses from diverse industries had very little variance. It is clear, therefore, that in M&A situations, human resource professionals are confronted with common challenges irrespective of industry.

NOTES

Clemente, Greenspan & Co., Inc.

Timing, Volume and Nature of Respondent Companies' Acquisitions

As stated, the role of human resources in acquisition planning and integration is changing rapidly. The activities of HR professionals in M&A transactions five years ago would not be reflective of the activities HR is now coordinating. An accurate picture of HR's current M&A responsibilities, therefore, could only be generated through feedback from HR professionals who have been involved in M&A in the recent past.

In this section, respondents were asked to indicate the frequency of their companies' M&A activities over the past year and a half. They were also asked to characterize the intent of those transactions. For example, a question was posed regarding the nature of the respondents' companies' transactions (e.g., whether the deals were done for strategic growth purposes – or strictly as a means of effecting cost-reduction synergies).

How many mergers and/or acquisitions has your company undertaken in the past 18 months?

Issue

Respondents were asked to offer their insights on transactions their companies undertook over an 18-month time period. This time frame was cited to allow respondents to assess the progress of past transactions and to indicate areas of responsibility that are undertaken at different points in the post-merger timetable. The 18-month time period was also used since, from an evaluative standpoint, the true success or failure of an M&A transaction is only apparent over time.

Findings

Thirty-nine percent (39%) of the respondents stated that their company had undertaken more than three mergers and/or acquisitions over the past 18 months. The majority, 51%, responded that they had undertaken between one and three mergers and/or acquisitions in this time period. And 10% reported that it had been at least 18 months since their company undertook its last transaction.

> **"Without a process in place, each time we acquire a company, we have to re-invent the wheel."**
>
> **Global VP, Human Resources**
> **Media and entertainment company**

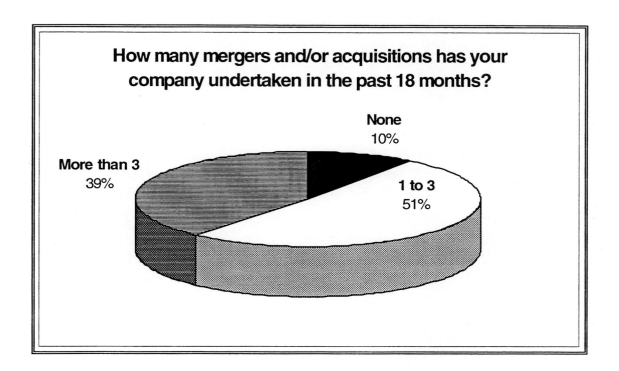

How many mergers and/or acquisitions has your company undertaken in the past 18 months?

None
10%

More than 3
39%

1 to 3
51%

Observations

The survey generated responses from HR professionals whose companies are actively involved in M&A. More than half (51%) of the respondents indicate that their company undertook one to three transactions in the last 18 months, and 39% conducted more than three deals (these companies can be considered highly acquisitive). Combining these statistics shows that fully 90% of the respondents have been involved in at least one M&A deal in the past 18 months. The remaining 10% provided input on their role in the M&A process, but their M&A experience was gained more than 18 months ago or when the respondents were employed elsewhere.

When was your most recent acquisition announced?

Issue

It was important to gauge the number of transactions respondents have been involved in the past, but also to determine how recent those transactions were. The goal was to ensure that the findings reflected feedback from HR professionals currently involved in M&A planning. A deal "announced" within the past three to six months may not have been finalized. Thus, the transaction is still in the planning stages. Conversely, deals announced over the past 12 months or longer, in most cases, have already closed and are now in the integration phase. It was necessary to solicit feedback from HR professionals participating at both ends of the M&A process.

Findings

Forty percent (40%) of the respondents indicated that their most recent acquisition was announced within the last three months. Fifteen percent (15%) of those surveyed cited the six-month mark, while 24% stated that their most recent acquisition had been announced within the last year (consequently, between 7 and 12 months ago). Twenty-one percent (21%) said that their most recent deal was announced more than a year ago.

> *"Every day I read about another acquisition and wonder, when will we be next?"*
>
> **Director, HR and Administration**
> **Publishing company**

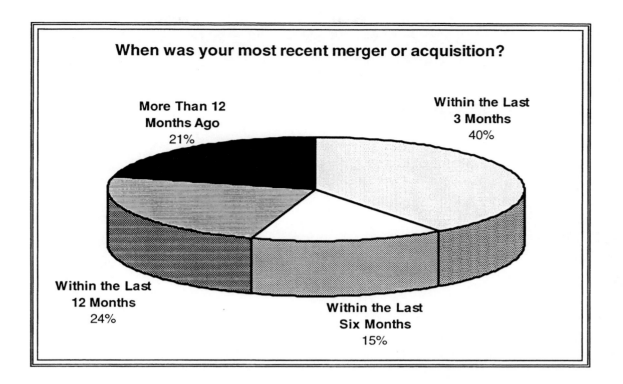

When was your most recent merger or acquisition?

More Than 12
Months Ago
21%

Within the Last
3 Months
40%

Within the Last
12 Months
24%

Within the Last
Six Months
15%

Observations

More than half of the respondents (55%) report that their company's most recent M&A transaction was undertaken in the last six months (40% plus 15%) – thus yielding insights from HR professionals whose companies may still be in the deal planning stages. Conversely, 45% of the respondents report being involved in deals over the past year or longer (24% plus 21%) – transactions that have likely been finalized. Taken together, the figures show a reasonable degree of balance of respondents now involved in both M&A planning and execution.

Describe the nature of your company's most recent acquisition.

Issue

This query sought to determine the nature and strategic rationale of the respondent companies' deals.

Findings

Seventy percent (77%) of the respondents said their most recent acquisition was one in which their company had acquired a domestic company.

Fifty percent (50%) of the respondents stated that their company had acquired a competitor ("horizontal merger"). Another 28% described their acquisition target as a supplier, distributor or manufacturer ("vertical merger"). The remaining 22% of respondents cited acquisitions in unrelated businesses or industries.

Less than one-third of all respondents (30%) said that the merger or acquisition was intended to create cost-reduction synergies (e.g., effecting economies of scale and scope). A majority of respondents (70%) cited the main reason their company had acquired or merged was to boost revenues.

> "We're acquiring to grow our business globally. HR's involvement in the process, I think, will be the key to success."
>
> **Human Resources Team Leader**
> **Business services firm**

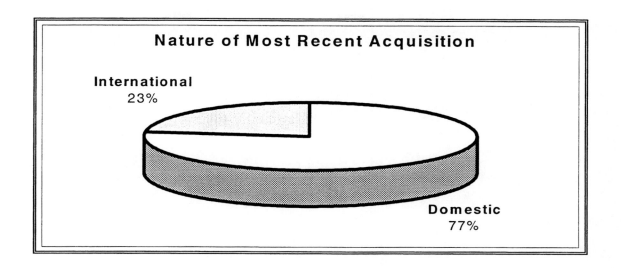

Nature of Most Recent Acquisition

International
23%

Domestic
77%

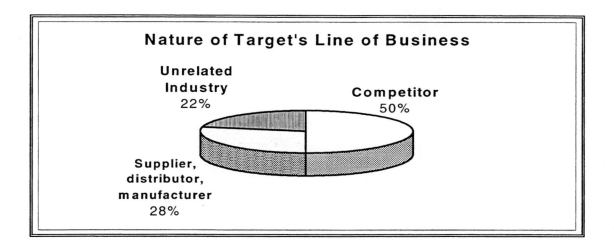

Nature of Target's Line of Business

Unrelated
Industry
22%

Competitor
50%

Supplier,
distributor,
manufacturer
28%

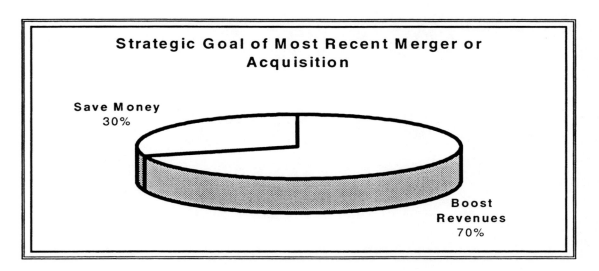

Strategic Goal of Most Recent Merger or Acquisition

Save Money
30%

Boost
Revenues
70%

Observations

In today's market, the vast preponderance of mergers and acquisitions have become strategic in nature. This is confirmed by the fact that 70% of the respondents cited *boosting revenues* as the main objective, which reinforces the market trend of deals shifting from a short-term cost savings orientation to one that is longer-term and revenue-based.

More than 78% of the respondents' acquisitions are in related industries. This, too, confirms the strategic nature of most M&A transactions today. When M&A occurs within the same industry or sector, companies generally have common understandings on which to build the integration platform. Although corporate cultures may be different, similarities in the language and processes of a particular industry help establish common ground, which can accelerate integration.

Evaluating Managerial Performance of Acquisition Planning and Integration

*R*espondents were asked to rate their company's performance in three key areas on which M&A success can be evaluated: addressing HR issues, communicating details of the acquisition to employees, and integrating the two companies.

These three issues, although discrete in their execution, interconnect in a number of areas. For example, effective communication is often a precursor to effective integration. Respondents were asked to rate management's level of effectiveness on a Likert scale ranging from 1 to 5 – with 1 being *ineffective* and 5 being *very effective*.

A noteworthy observation related to the large number of "3s" – signaling an unwillingness of respondents to categorize their company's efforts as decidedly effective. The fact that total scoring exceeded the middle point, however, indicated respondents' overall positivism toward their companies' performance.

Two other questions were posed to solicit feedback on the respondent companies' M&A performance. These related to employees' attitudes toward the merger six months after its completion. Here, the research hypothesis was that the more positive employees' attitudes, the more effective management's integration and cultural alignment initiatives were.

Please rate your company's performance in its most recent acquisition:

Addressing HR Issues

Issue

Asking HR directors — as opposed to senior or operations management — how well their companies addressed HR issues was viewed as a means of generating the most accurate insights on managerial performance in this area.

Findings

On a scale basis, the average response was 3.6.

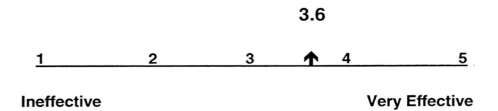

3.6

1   2   3   ↑   4   5

Ineffective   **Very Effective**

From a percentage standpoint, 45% of respondents rated their company's performance positively: *effective* (37%) or *very effective* (8%); 36% of the respondents were neutral; 19% (15% plus 4%) categorized their company's performance as somewhat *ineffective.*

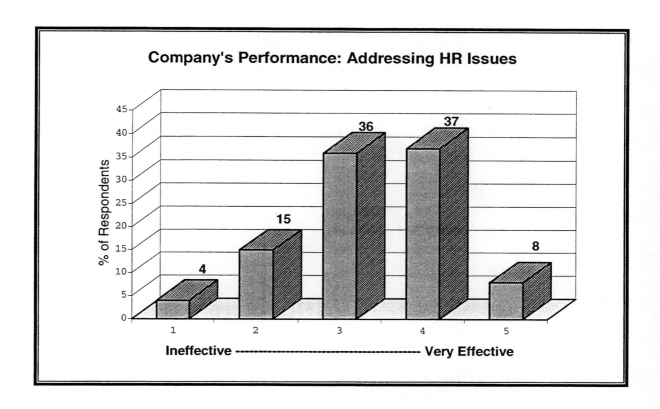

Company's Performance: Addressing HR Issues

% of Respondents

45
40
35
30
25
20
15
10
5
0

4 — 1
15 — 2
36 — 3
37 — 4
8 — 5

Ineffective -- Very Effective

Observations

A two-thirds majority of respondents felt their companies have been *effective* or *very effective* in addressing HR issues. This is encouraging. However, the fact that one-third of all companies are *not* effectively addressing HR issues clearly indicates that there is room for improvement.

Please rate your company's performance in its most recent acquisition:

Communicating Details of the Acquisition to the Merged Company's Employees

Issue

HR's involvement in employee communications is of paramount importance. Within the context of M&A, the merged firm's vision must be clearly and persuasively communicated to the new employee base — and time-sensitive information of an administrative and operational nature must be effectively imparted.

Findings

On a scale basis, the average response was 3.72.

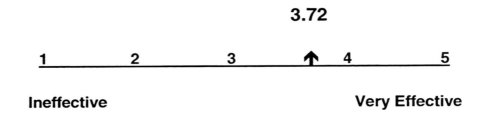

From a percentage standpoint, 41% of respondents rated their company's performance in this area as *effective* and 18% indicated *very effective*; 29% of the respondents were neutral; 12% of the respondents characterized their company's performance as *ineffective*.

CLEMENTE, GREENSPAN & CO., INC.

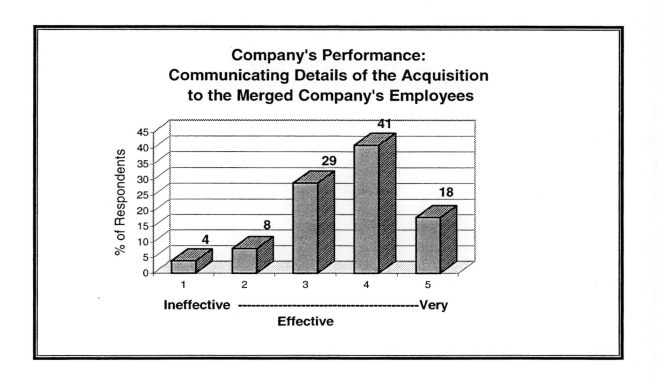

Observations

More than half of the respondents feel their companies did an effective job of employee communication. Yet a very sizable percentage of them feel management did not. HR professionals clearly recognize that, in order to ensure employee retention and motivation, communications must be consistent, informative and compelling throughout all phases of the acquisition process.

Please rate your company's performance in its most recent acquisition:

Integrating the Two Companies

Issue

The effectiveness of a company's integration program is a strong predictor of the likelihood of long-term success of a merger or acquisition.

Findings

On a scale basis, the average response was 3.3.

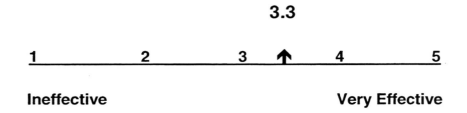

From a percentage standpoint, 45% of respondents rated their company's performance as somewhat effective: (37% cited *effective*, 8% cited *very effective*). Thirty-six percent (36%) were neutral; 19% – almost one out of five – characterized their company's performance as *ineffective*.

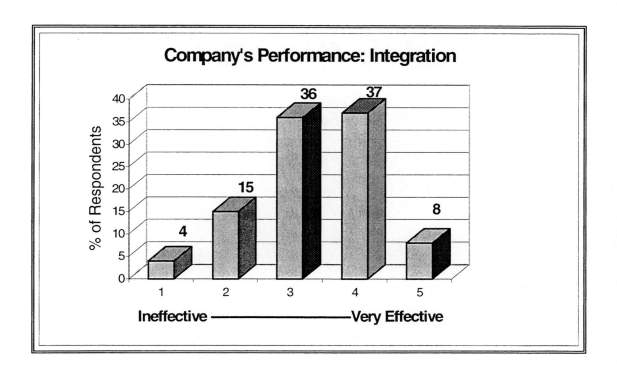

Company's Performance: Integration

% of Respondents

| Ineffective ——————— Very Effective |

Observations

The neutral ranking was again very prominent, highlighting the lack of conviction that more than half of all respondents have regarding the effectiveness of their company's integration performance. Effective integration, by all accounts, marks the difference between a merger succeeding or failing. HR has the power to influence this by taking a strong role in specific integration activities. (But, as the responses to questions on HR's current M&A activities will point out, less than half of the respondents are involved in the *tactical execution* of several key integration activities – see page 81.)

Rate *your* employees' attitudes toward the merger/acquisition within the first six months of the transaction:

Issue

Employee attitudes, post-merger, are directly influenced by internal communication and overall integration planning and implementation. Workers' attitudes, however, typically vary depending on whether their company is the acquirer or the acquired.

Findings

Sixty-five percent (65%) of respondents felt their employees viewed the merger or acquisition as positive; 27% defined their employees' attitude as ambivalent; 8% felt that employees viewed the transaction negatively.

> *"HR should be the driver of the (M&A) process. Each employee needs to feel comfortable about what will or won't happen as it pertains to them. This part must be accomplished first before employees can embrace any new operational and cultural changes."*
>
> Senior VP, Human Resources
> Healthcare provider

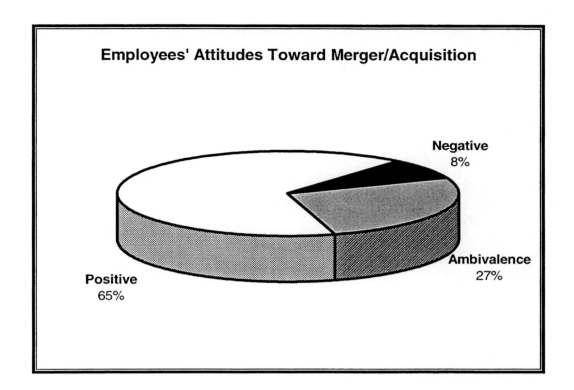

Employees' Attitudes Toward Merger/Acquisition

Negative 8%

Ambivalence 27%

Positive 65%

Observations

A surprisingly high percentage of respondents reported employee acceptance of the M&A transaction. Still, one-third felt their own employees did not view the merger positively. This indicates a significant level of discontent – which could either be attributed to companies not effectively communicating the benefits of the transaction to employees; employees not embracing the strategic rationale of the deal; or to workers' negative reactions to a major post-merger corporate restructuring (including layoffs).

Rate the _acquired_ employees' attitudes toward the merger/acquisition within the first six months of the transaction:

Issue

Respondents were asked to rate the acquired employees' attitudes – whose sentiments toward a transaction often vary dramatically in contrast to employees in the acquiring firm.

Findings

Fifty-seven percent (57%) of respondents felt the acquired employees viewed the merger or acquisition _positively_; 27% defined their attitude as _ambivalent_; 16% felt that employees viewed the transaction _negatively_.

> _"Not adequately attending to people issues is one of the main reasons for acquisition failures."_
>
> **Senior VP, Human Resources**
> **Consumer electronics manufacturer**

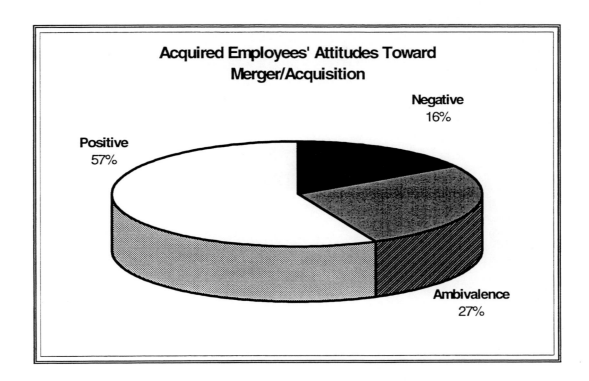

Acquired Employees' Attitudes Toward Merger/Acquisition

Negative
16%

Positive
57%

Ambivalence
27%

Observations

It was expected — yet noteworthy — that there would be a difference in sentiment between acquiring and acquired employees. In fact, there was a 100% increase in those viewing the transaction as negative (16% of the respondents reported that the acquired employees viewed the transaction negatively; 8% of respondents reported employees in the acquiring organization as viewing the deal negatively). All told, more than four out of every 10 respondents felt acquired employees did not view the merger or acquisition positively. Negative sentiments toward the acquirer are to be expected in the wake of a merger or acquisition, particularly when massive changes or downsizings are leveled at the acquired firm. The solutions are increased communications, employee sensing, training and reward and recognition programs.

NOTES

Critical Post-Merger Issues

The close of a merger or acquisition creates immediate challenges to senior management, in general, and to HR professionals, in particular. The survey sought to garner respondents' feedback on the issues they viewed as most critical in the wake of an acquisition.

Respondents were asked to indicate which two of the following issues required immediate attention upon a transaction's close:

- ➤ Communication
- ➤ Potential culture clashes
- ➤ Employee morale
- ➤ Products and services
- ➤ Revenue generation
- ➤ Duplication of job functions
- ➤ Staffing
- ➤ Compensation

Some of these issues are decidedly human resource-oriented. Two of them – *products and services* and *revenue generation* – are outside the realm of HR, but pose direct challenges to HR from a personnel and organizational development standpoint.

What are the two most important issues that must be addressed in the wake of a merger/acquisition?

Issue - Communication

All post-merger integration programs have as a central component regular communications to the merged company's employee base. Communications are necessary to impart information needed to get the combined workforces moving toward the organization's strategic goals. Additionally, communications are needed to begin effecting long-term alignment of disparate corporate cultures.

Findings

Seventy percent (70%) of the survey respondents cited "communication" as being one of the two most critical issues after the close of a merger or acquisition.

> *"Human resource professionals must play a major role in all aspects (of the M&A process): due diligence through post-merger planning. Communication is key."*
>
> **Director of Benefits**
> **Beverage company**

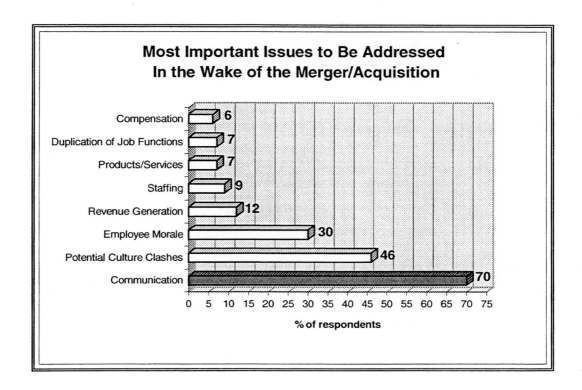

Most Important Issues to Be Addressed In the Wake of the Merger/Acquisition

Compensation — 6
Duplication of Job Functions — 7
Products/Services — 7
Staffing — 9
Revenue Generation — 12
Employee Morale — 30
Potential Culture Clashes — 46
Communication — 70

% of respondents

Observations

Communication was cited by the most respondents as being a crucial post-deal issue. This is probably due to two factors: many deal failures that have been chronicled in the press cited faulty communication as a main failing of the integration program. Second, HR professionals recognize the criticality of communication in maximizing productivity and facilitating any and all forms of organizational change. HR must recognize that post-merger communications, however, pose a unique change-management challenge. Post-merger integration is a long-term undertaking. Consequently, communications must be carefully tailored for all phases of the integration process.

What are the two most important issues that must be addressed in the wake of a merger/acquisition?

Issue - Potential Culture Clashes

It is imperative to understand the dynamics and attributes of different corporate cultures in order to avoid the *culture clashes* that have killed many a strategically sound merger or acquisition. This entails evaluating the process- and personnel-related components of corporate culture to identify the likelihood of post-merger conflicts among employees and to devise measures to effect speedy integration.

Findings

A little less than half (46%) of the respondents cited "potential culture clashes" as a key area of attention upon close of the M&A transaction.

"It's our job to develop strategies/tactics to help management minimize HR-related risks. These include risks of both a financial and cultural nature."

HR Director
Consumer products company

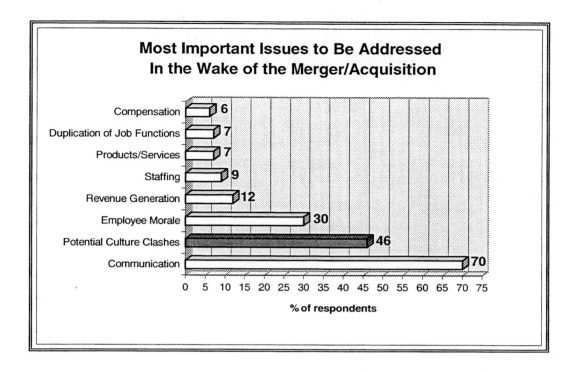

**Most Important Issues to Be Addressed
In the Wake of the Merger/Acquisition**

Issue	% of respondents
Compensation	6
Duplication of Job Functions	7
Products/Services	7
Staffing	9
Revenue Generation	12
Employee Morale	30
Potential Culture Clashes	46
Communication	70

% of respondents

Observations

The devastating consequences of culture clash have been a well-publicized reason for many failed mergers and acquisitions. Perhaps more than any other variable, it has been cited as a key problem area that must be addressed in pre-merger planning and post-merger integration – which explains why almost half of the respondents cite the importance of this issue. Spotting potential culture clashes must be done early in the acquisition planning process. That is, target company screening should include cultural considerations. Moreover, a detailed examination of an M&A target's culture should comprise a main element of HR due diligence. Culture clash, however, may arise even in situations where it appeared it would not. HR must recognize this possibility and focus on cultural alignment once a target has been identified. Early awareness of a potential culture clash will provide HR ample time to develop more culturally focused integration strategies.

What are the most important issues that must be addressed in the wake of a merger/acquisition?

Issue - Employee Morale

The organizational climate after a major merger or acquisition is often characterized by employee uncertainty and fear as firmwide staffing and departmental decisions are being made. Employee morale typically drops in the weeks and months following the transaction's close. So, too, does productivity as enthusiasm ebbs. The challenge to HR professionals is minimizing the downturn in employee morale – and swiftly taking steps to restore it as part of the post-merger integration game plan.

Findings

Thirty percent (30%) viewed "employee morale" as being one of the most important issues that must first be addressed in the wake of an acquisition.

> "HR must be ready and fast-acting to evaluate the HR costs and liabilities related to benefits and compensation. Once the acquisition is made, HR must make quick assessments of employee morale, organizational structure, and personnel-related policies and procedures."
>
> **Manager of Human Resources**
> **Pharmaceuticals company**

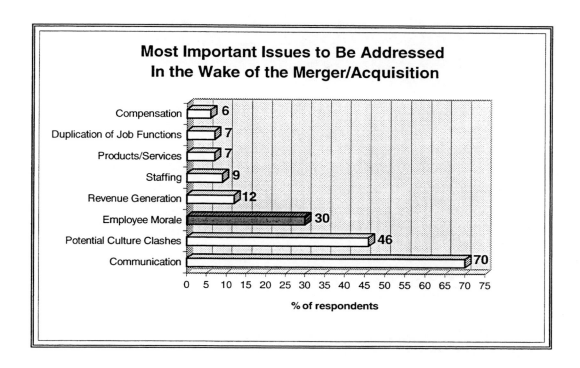

Observations

Less than one-third of respondents see employee morale as being a major post-deal issue. In actuality, the detrimental impact low employee morale can have on post-merger integration initiatives means HR professionals must evaluate and mitigate decreased morale quickly. The challenge involves not only determining that morale is low, but ascertaining the reasons why. Employee sensing – via focus groups and other research methods – is necessary. This research should be conducted not once, but rather periodically over the course of the integration timetable. Most important, the research must be acted upon. Specific measures must quickly be taken to heighten morale by lessening employees' fears and concerns as soon as HR becomes aware of them.

What are the most important issues that must be addressed in the wake of a merger/ acquisition?

Issue - Products and Services

One of the most pressing challenges of post-merger integration is aligning two companies' product and service lines. (This is a key factor in most "horizontal" mergers, in which companies in the same or similar industries combine.) Product line duplications must be identified and eliminated to reduce costs and to maximize sales. A merged company that is slow in finalizing its product and service offerings also risks confusing and alienating customers, suppliers and distributors.

Findings

Seven percent (7%) of the respondents cited "products and services" as one of the two most important issues to be addressed upon close of the M&A transaction.

> *"Even in a product-driven acquisition, HR must take a leadership role"*
>
> **Global Director, Human Resources**
> **Chemicals manufacturer**

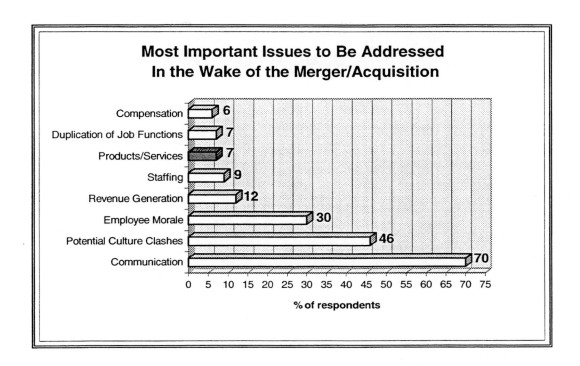

Most Important Issues to Be Addressed In the Wake of the Merger/Acquisition

Compensation — 6
Duplication of Job Functions — 7
Products/Services — 7
Staffing — 9
Revenue Generation — 12
Employee Morale — 30
Potential Culture Clashes — 46
Communication — 70

% of respondents

Observations

The fact that HR professionals typically have little or no involvement in managerial decisions on products and services explains the low level of importance placed on this issue. Product and service line decisions fall outside the domain of HR professionals. But decisions relative to staffing selections and the physical deployment of personnel *do* come under HR's purview. From this standpoint, HR professionals should be involved in product and service decisions in terms of personnel assessment and selection (e.g., for R&D, product managers), general facilities planning, and determining the personnel costs associated with ongoing product management and distribution.

What are the most important issues that must be addressed in the wake of a merger/acquisition?

Issue - Revenue Generation

Generating top-line revenue gains is a key determinant of successful mergers and acquisitions. Transactions that are focused solely on cost-cutting tend to result in only short-term financial gains for the combined company. Transactions that have as their foundation multiple ways to generate revenues over the near-, middle- and long-term have significantly higher chances of succeeding and creating sustained shareholder value.

Findings

Twelve percent (12%) of the respondents felt "revenue generation" is a critical issue for HR professionals in the post-merger environment.

> *"HR's key areas of responsibility in M&A should be employee communication, cultural integration, staffing and compensation — all in support of a positive integration and leading toward revenue generation."*
>
> **Director, Compensation & Benefits**
> **Industrial products company**

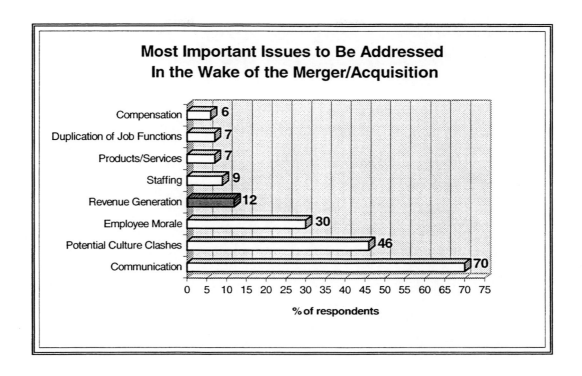

**Most Important Issues to Be Addressed
In the Wake of the Merger/Acquisition**

Compensation — 6
Duplication of Job Functions — 7
Products/Services — 7
Staffing — 9
Revenue Generation — 12
Employee Morale — 30
Potential Culture Clashes — 46
Communication — 70

% of respondents

Observations

The low level of significance respondents placed on "revenue generation" mirrors the lack of importance they place on broader "product and service" issues. HR professionals evidently feel they should have minimal involvement in supporting these marketing- and sales-related areas. In fact, HR can contribute value here and should play a major role. In the wake of a merger or acquisition, staffing decisions must be based on the skills needed to grow the merged firm and bolster its competitive standing. (This is addressed in greater detail in the observations on "staffing.") However, that is only one area where HR can support revenue-generation initiatives. Others include employee communications and training and development which – when focused on supporting corporate growth programs – can help the merged company effectively meet current and evolving customer needs.

What are the most important issues that must be addressed in the wake of a merger/acquisition?

Issue - Duplication of Job Functions

Mergers of horizontally aligned companies usually present situations where there is duplication of personnel in administrative and operational areas. Cost-reduction synergies through personnel cutbacks are sought, at least to some degree, in virtually every such merger or acquisition. Eliminating redundant personnel and their attendant benefits costs is usually the largest area of cost savings in mergers of companies that are structured similarly.

Findings

Seven percent (7%) of the respondents cited "duplication of job functions" as an important post-merger integration issue.

> *"HR must work directly with management to make their assessment and selection process as effective as possible."*
>
> **VP, Human Resources**
> **Professional services firm**

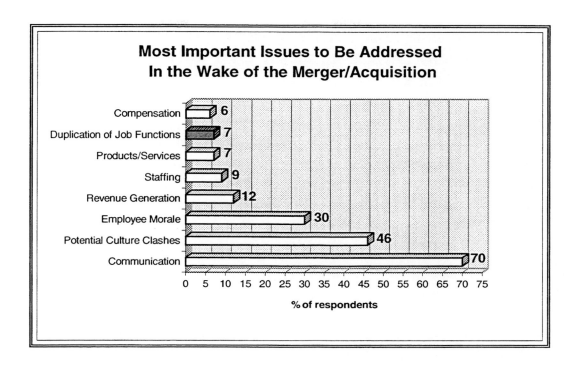

Observations

A surprisingly low number of respondents acknowledge the importance of this issue. Identifying the extent to which there is duplication in job functions helps in quantifying cost-savings that can be attained post–merger. But there is an inherent challenge to personnel cost-reduction opportunities. HR must ensure that management takes a disciplined approach to head-count reductions; cuts cannot be made indiscriminately lest they complicate near-term operations or the merged company's ability to undertake longer-term strategic initiatives.

What are the most important issues that must be addressed in the wake of a merger/acquisition?

Issue - Staffing

Post-merger personnel staffing decisions should be based on a fundamental determination: what skills must be resident in the merged company in order for it to successfully achieve the objectives of the M&A transaction. A "skills based" approach to staffing must be undertaken. This entails weighing the needs of the combined firm from the standpoint of the "value drivers" sought through the transaction. In other words, staffing must directly support the strategic goals of the combined company and the tactics it will employ to achieve those objectives.

Findings

Nine percent (9%) of the respondents view "staffing" as a strategically significant post-merger issue.

> *"HR must be involved from the very first stages to make recommendations to management on whether to proceed with the acquisition from a staffing, organizational structure, culture and integration standpoint."*
>
> **VP, Compensation and Benefits**
> **Industrial products company**

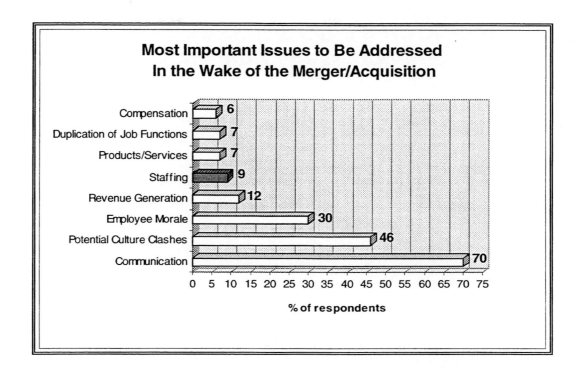

**Most Important Issues to Be Addressed
In the Wake of the Merger/Acquisition**

Issue	% of respondents
Compensation	6
Duplication of Job Functions	7
Products/Services	7
Staffing	9
Revenue Generation	12
Employee Morale	30
Potential Culture Clashes	46
Communication	70

% of respondents

Observations

The extremely low level of importance placed on staffing by respondents is consistent with the lack of importance they placed on "duplication of job functions." These issues are directly related. The statistics generated confirm that relationship. As stated, post-merger job cuts and staffing decisions must not be made indiscriminately. HR must address the quantitative and qualitative considerations inherent in the process. Quantitatively, HR must help management determine the number of people that will populate the combined company's staffing ranks. Qualitatively, HR must coordinate an empirical, scientifically based approach to identifying the company's requisite skills at both the corporate and individual business unit levels.

What are the most important issues that must be addressed in the wake of a merger/ acquisition?

Issue - Compensation

Companies compensate their employees in different ways, at different levels, and at different time intervals. Aligning compensation programs – and the performance appraisal measures and systems on which compensation decisions are based – represents a primary post-merger integration task. What's more, the differences that may exist between merging companies' compensation programs are a key area of investigation during HR due diligence.

Findings

Six percent (6%) of respondents cited "compensation" as one of the two most significant issues to address post-merger.

> *"In our business, we don't transact with assets, we transact with people. That's why HR is so critical."*
>
> **Director of Compensation**
> **Mail order catalogue retailer**

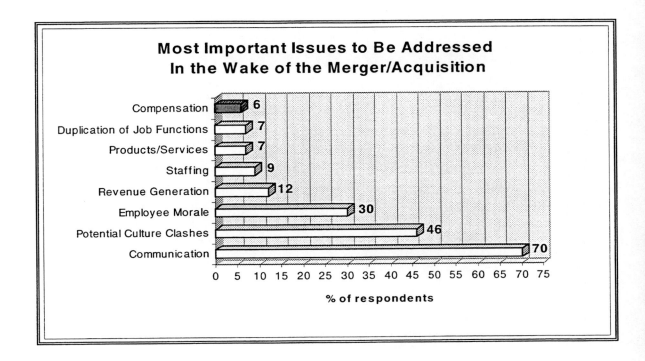

Most Important Issues to Be Addressed In the Wake of the Merger/Acquisition

Issue	% of respondents
Compensation	6
Duplication of Job Functions	7
Products/Services	7
Staffing	9
Revenue Generation	12
Employee Morale	30
Potential Culture Clashes	46
Communication	70

% of respondents

Observations

An extremely low level of importance was placed on compensation by the respondents. Yet, compensation policies must be finalized as soon as possible after the transaction's close for two reasons. First, compensation and benefits are an acquired employee's single greatest concern; the first questions HR will have to field will likely be in this area. Second, marked disparities in compensation between employees from the merging companies can foster organization-wide resentment that can hamper integration and cultural alignment. In an M&A situation, compensation program design means more than ensuring equality between the combining employee bases. It also means that financial rewards may prove valuable to employees who are demonstrating the collegiality and teamwork needed to effect integration.

HR's Current Role in Acquisition Planning and Integration

*T*o determine the nature of respondents' involvement in their companies' M&A program, the survey asked them whether or not they participate in 10 chronological activities that comprise the acquisition planning and integration process:

1. Acquisition strategy

2. Screening target companies

3. Conducting due diligence

4. Planning post-merger integration

5. Implementing post-merger integration

6. Employee communications

7. Employee sensing

8. Assessment and selection

9. Training and development

10. Managing organizational/cultural change

The responses provided a clear indication of the areas on which HR professionals focus most in corporate mergers and acquisitions. The findings also pointed up several critical activities in which HR is currently playing only a limited role.

HR's Involvement in the Overall M&A Process

Initially, this question sought to determine the extent to which respondents are involved in the five basic phases of the M&A process: acquisition strategy development; target company screening; conducting due diligence; integration planning; and integration implementation. Integration implementation is a multi-faceted process. For this reason, respondents' roles in each of the discrete activities comprising integration execution are discussed later in this section.

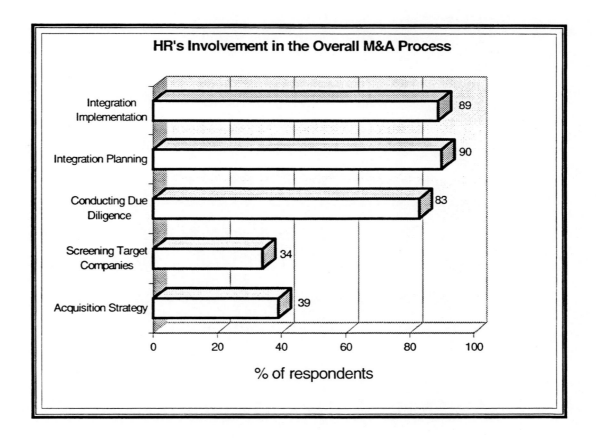

Indicate the M&A activities in which your HR department is typically involved:

Working with Management to Support Acquisition Strategy

Issue

M&A is driven by strategic decisions by a company on how it chooses to grow. The first stage in this decision-making process is identifying one or more strategic drivers – attainable through M&A – that focus the company's efforts in a particular growth direction. In M&A, human asset considerations (e.g., key knowledge workers to acquire) must be foremost in acquisition strategy and identifying potential target companies.

Findings

Less than half – closer to two-thirds – (39%) of the HR professionals surveyed report working with management to support acquisition strategy development.

"HR should be part of the team that assesses, evaluates and integrates acquisitions ... and should be a full strategic partner (with management) to make sure the M&A transaction is a long-term success."

VP, Human Resources
Business services firm

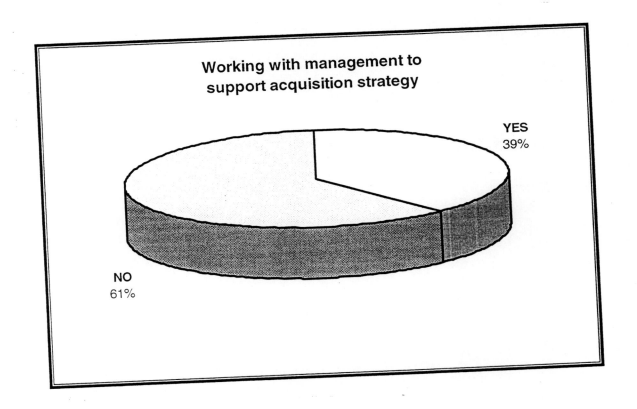

**Working with management to
support acquisition strategy**

YES
39%

NO
61%

Observations

HR is playing a relatively small role in this, the initial phase of the M&A process. The statistics point up the fact that, at the highest level and in the earliest stages, decisions on the type of people to be acquired – and the tactics necessary to retain and leverage those human assets post-merger – are being left to managers outside the realm of HR. Companies failing to involve HR in this stage of the acquisition process leave themselves open to a major potential problem. Namely, buying corporate assets without actually acquiring the types of people and skill sets required to attain post-merger growth objectives.

Indicate the M&A activities in which your HR department is typically involved:

Evaluating or Screening Target Companies

Issue

Once the corporate M&A strategy has been devised, the next activity is identifying and screening one or more companies that represent possible merger or acquisition partners. Effective screening is imperative from an HR standpoint. A given company might, on the surface, appear to meet management's strategic criteria. However, evaluating the company from a human resources perspective might reveal fundamental shortcomings (e.g., in terms of skills composition) or insurmountable cultural obstacles.

Findings

Approximately one-third (34%) of those surveyed are involved in evaluating or screening target companies.

"Advisor, fact-finder, 'devil's advocate' to management –

that's the role HR should play in the M&A process."

Corporate VP, Human Resources
Financial services firm

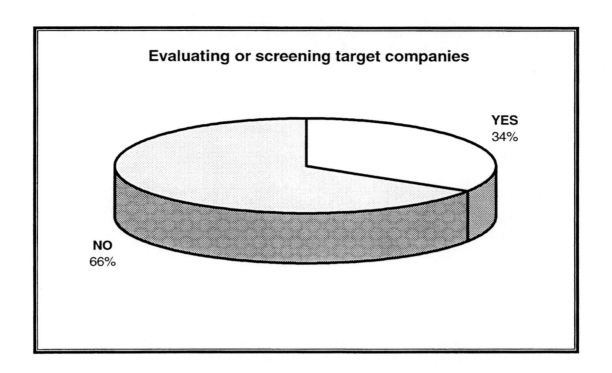

Evaluating or screening target companies

YES
34%

NO
66%

Observations

Two-thirds of the HR professionals participating in the study do not contribute to this critical pre-deal activity. This points up a major failing of management. By not involving HR, there is a low likelihood of effective pre-deal assessments of the human and cultural aspects of a given acquisition opportunity. An organization that proceeds along the M&A course without insight on these matters forces HR to overcome post-deal problems that could have been completely avoided through pre-deal screening.

Indicate the M&A activities in which your HR department is typically involved:

Conducting Due Diligence

Issue

Once a target has been identified, approached, and an offer made, the detailed investigative process known as *due diligence* begins. Traditional due diligence involves examinations by financial, legal, accounting and tax experts designed to unearth liabilities and place a value on the target's assets. More forward-thinking companies include HR and marketing professionals to perform a more thorough analysis. Their inclusion helps the due diligence team arrive at a more accurate valuation of the target company, and better defines the crucial people and revenue generation issues that will determine the likelihood of the deal's long-term success.

Findings

Eighty-three percent (83%) of those surveyed play a role in their companies' due diligence investigations.

"Our organization isn't there yet. But, hopefully, HR will someday be a member of the due diligence team and a participant in acquisition strategy. Right now, HR is the implementer of post-acquisition assimilation programs. In the future, I hope we'll be playing a greater role in evaluating the (target) organization and proposing appropriate changes in the structure of the merged company."

VP, Human Resources
Consumer products manufacturer

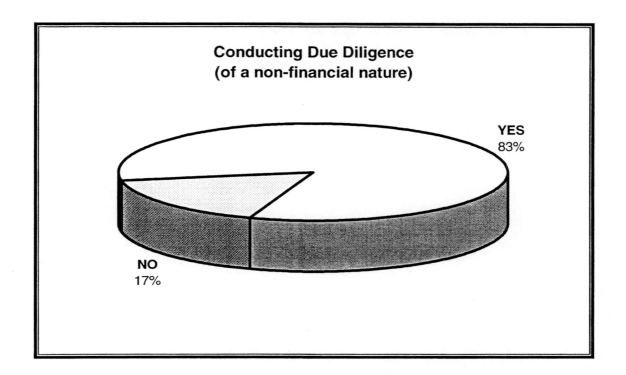

**Conducting Due Diligence
(of a non-financial nature)**

YES
83%

NO
17%

Observations

The tremendously high level of involvement of HR illustrates management's recognition of the criticality of exploring cultural and broader people issues in the due diligence phase. This was the most encouraging aspect of the entire study. HR is evidently working alongside other functions – such as finance – to identify potential financial liabilities (e.g., under-funded retirement plans). HR is also being asked to evaluate other key HR-related issues, such as a target company's compensation, staffing and benefit structures.

Indicate the M&A activities in which your HR department is typically involved:

Planning Post-Merger Integration

Issue

Immediately after the due diligence process is completed, the action plan for post-transaction integration is developed. Historically, this is where HR has first gotten involved in the M&A process.

Findings

Ninety percent (90%) of the respondents report being involved in planning post-merger integration.

"HR's primary role is in identifying the priority people issues that must be managed to make the integration successful."

Director of Benefits
International banking company

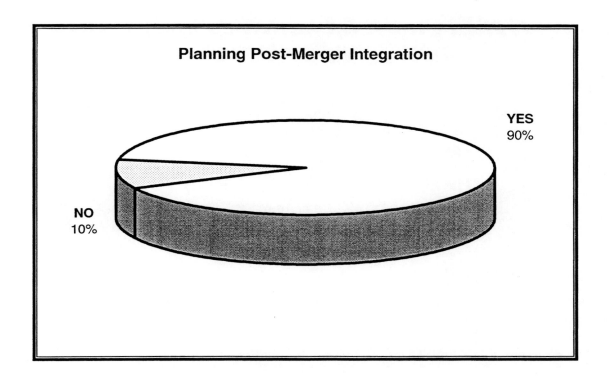

Planning Post-Merger Integration

YES
90%

NO
10%

Observations

Nine out of 10 HR professionals participating in the study are involved in planning post-merger integration. And, as the previous statistics indicated, HR is becoming broadly involved in due diligence as well. The two phases go hand-in-hand: effective due diligence points up integration challenges and imperatives. However, when integration planning is HR's point of entry in the M&A process, then a substantial amount of catching up will be necessary – and a series of avoidable, personnel-related problems may well have arisen.

Indicate the M&A activities in which your HR department is typically involved:

Implementing Post-Merger Integration

Issue

Planning post-merger integration sets the stage for its implementation. The managers planning integration activities should be directly involved in their execution.

Findings

Eighty-nine percent (89%) of the respondents report being directly involved in implementing post-merger integration.

"HR should be a critical component of both the target company evaluation and due diligence phases ... in addition to 'cleaning up the mess' post-merger."

Manager of Human Resources
Publishing company

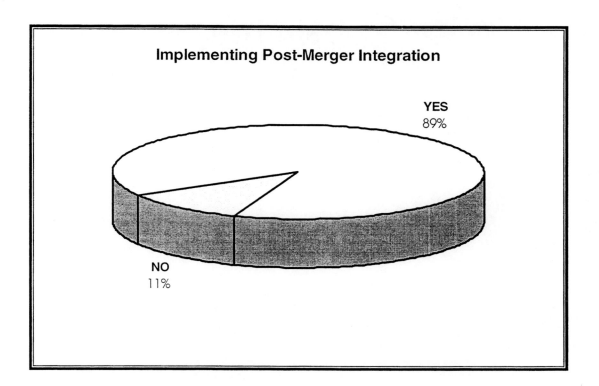

Implementing Post-Merger Integration

YES
89%

NO
11%

Observations

Reinforcing their extensive involvement in integration planning, nearly nine out of 10 HR professionals play a key role in implementing the strategy. Keep in mind, however, that there are many discrete activities falling under the umbrella of integration implementation. The study broke down the various components of integration implementation and asked HR professionals to cite their department's involvement in each. These findings follow.

NOTES

Post-Merger Integration:

Tactical Execution

Within the context of post–merger integration are five core activities that are typically driven by human resource professionals: assessment and selection, communications, employee sensing, training and development, and change management.

Although an overwhelming majority of respondents cited their involvement in post–merger integration, this section breaks down integration into its discrete tactical components. Respondents were asked to indicate their involvement in each of the five core activities.

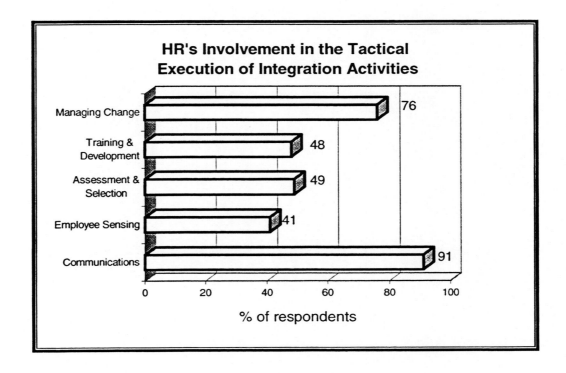

Indicate the M&A activities in which your HR department is typically involved:

Employee Communications

Issue

Communications are, without question, one of the most important activities in the realm of integration implementation. Disseminating information on the merged firm's new vision – as well as information on new policies, procedures, and programs – is a critical task that begins prior to the official announcement and continues through all phases of the integration program.

Findings

Ninety-one percent (91%) of the respondents report direct involvement in merger-related communication programs.

"Besides heading the communications and all employee-related matters, HR should play a key role on the M&A team to ensure overall success."

VP, Human Resources
Industrial manufacturing company

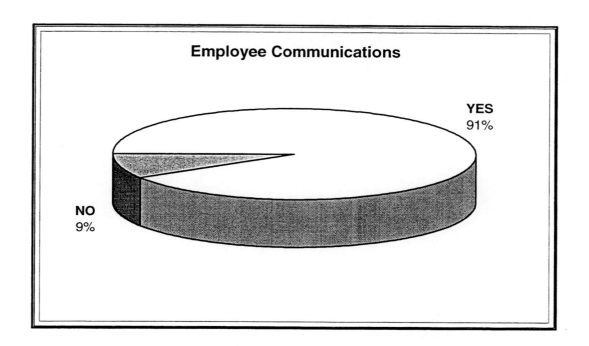

Employee Communications

YES
91%

NO
9%

Observations

Communication was the integration activity most frequently cited by the respondents. Post-merger communications are key to unifying disparate workforces and aligning corporate cultures. And whether communications are crafted by benefit consultants, or in-house marketing or corporate communication departments, HR professionals are playing an active role. Communications are designed to inform, influence and inspire *people*. HR professionals must remain instrumental in shaping communication messages since they best understand the intended recipients of those messages.

Indicate the M&A activities in which your HR department is typically involved:

Employee Sensing

Issue

As the merger process proceeds, HR must receive feedback from all employees in order to plan communications, training, and change-management initiatives. Employee feedback drives programs designed to retain, motivate and train workers. Formal sensing mechanisms (e.g., focus groups, surveys and one-on-one interviews) can provide HR with the critical insight it needs to guide integration and cultural alignment.

Findings

Forty-one percent (41%) of the survey respondents report involvement in employee sensing programs.

"Of particular importance is evaluating unique cultural issues, and planning and monitoring the effectiveness of the overall communication effort. This includes 'listening' to all employees affected by the merger or acquisition."

Senior VP, Human Resources
Hospitality company

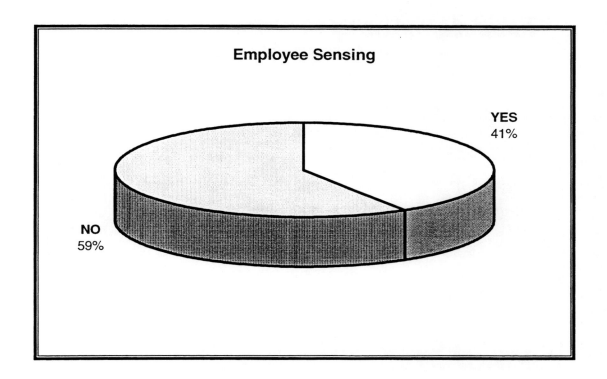

Employee Sensing

YES
41%

NO
59%

Observations

In more than half (59%) of the companies queried, eliciting feedback from the employee base is *not* a priority. Failing to gauge employee feelings can be extremely dangerous. Without monitoring employee attitudes after a merger or acquisition, HR professionals will not detect negative sentiments that may be emerging and which can hamper attempts at integration and the melding of corporate cultures. HR must lead the change-management initiative that is M&A. If HR professionals are not proactively soliciting employee feedback, then change-management measures may become flawed in either their design or execution.

Indicate the M&A activities in which your HR department is typically involved:

Assessment and Selection

Issue

HR must play a lead role in helping management identify the core competencies necessary to realize the strategic drivers of an M&A transaction. A disciplined "skills-based" approach is needed to design job specifications and to identify the experiential attributes and behavioral traits required of employees at different levels of the merged company.

Findings

Forty-nine percent (49%) of the HR professionals queried are involved in post-merger employee assessment and selection.

"It's particularly important for HR to make assessments of the potential acquired company's management."

VP and Human Resource Director
Design and engineering company

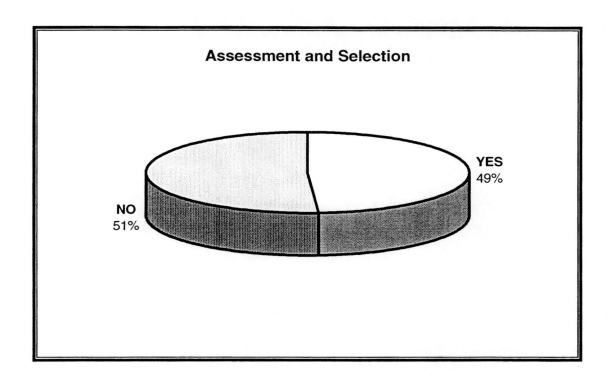

Assessment and Selection

YES
49%

NO
51%

Observations

HR directors are broadly involved in integration implementation, but more than half of those surveyed say it is not in the area of assessment and selection. The fact is, after the closing of a deal, there will likely be overlaps of senior executives and managers lower down in the hierarchy. Duplicative positions must obviously be eliminated. But if broader job cuts are envisioned as a cost-reduction synergy, personnel and staffing decisions must be made carefully. Managements must realize that post-merger assessment and selection directly impacts the merged company's ability to achieve its growth objectives.

Indicate the M&A activities in which your HR department is typically involved:

Training and Development

Issue

Training is another activity that is central to effective integration and cultural alignment. Training is needed to impart information of a policy and procedural nature. It is also beneficial in its ability to be motivational and to serve as a catalyst in building teamwork and collegiality between combining workforces.

Findings

Forty-eight percent (48%) of all respondents are involved in M&A-related training and development.

> *"Effective integration requires education. Education comes from training. Training ensures that everyone stays on the same page. Without it, the process will fall apart."*
> **VP, Human Resources**
> **Consumer products manufacturer**

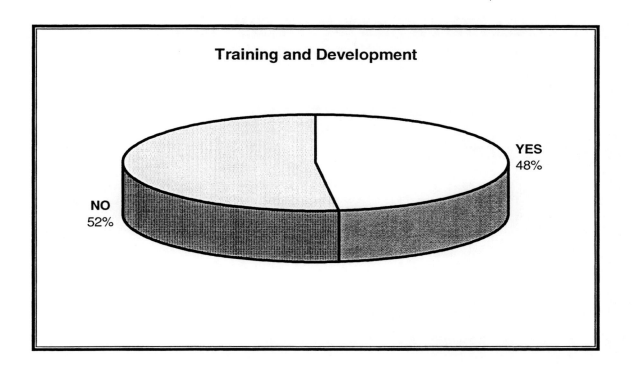

Training and Development

YES
48%

NO
52%

Observations

Training is an area in which HR is clearly not playing as large a role as it should be, with only less than half of the respondents (48%) citing involvement. Post-merger training must include orientation classes and interactive workshops that are scheduled at different points in the post-merger timetable. It is essential to view training not as a one-time event. Rather, it should be comprised of an ongoing series of activities designed to facilitate and expedite integration.

Indicate the M&A activities in which your HR department is typically involved:

Managing Organizational/Cultural Change

Issue

Clearly, a merger or acquisition represents the ultimate change-management initiative. A corporate combination of virtually any scope alters the workings of the companies involved. HR must assume responsibility for shepherding the change-management process. Over the long-term it must guide the evolution of the new company's culture. In the near term, HR must build morale and effect productivity in a highly volatile work environment.

Findings

Seventy-six percent (76%) of the HR professionals who responded are involved in managing organizational/ cultural change.

"HR can play an important role in helping the organization cope with change."

Director, Corporate Management and Employee Development

Financial services company

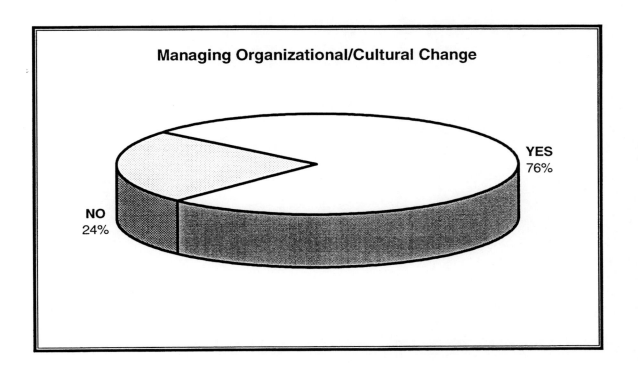

Managing Organizational/Cultural Change

YES
76%

NO
24%

Observations

A solid majority of respondents participate in merger-related organizational change-management initiatives. However, it is curious that, despite this substantive level of involvement, a minority of respondents report involvement in the earlier question of employee sensing and research (41%). Employee feedback must drive change-management strategies. That is, workers' attitudes must be clearly defined if the merged company is to design change-management programs that effectively alter beliefs and behaviors for integration purposes.

NOTES

The Importance of HR in the M&A Process:

A Self-Assessment

*T*his portion of the survey was designed to solicit feedback on the importance respondents placed on HR's involvement in five core activities comprising the merger and acquisition process:

1. Working with management to support acquisition strategy

2. Evaluating target companies/screening candidates

3. Working on the due diligence team

4. Planning post-merger integration

5. Implementing post-merger integration

The survey questions were structured using a Likert scale ranking of 1 to 5, with 1 being *not important* and 5 being *very important.* The questions were designed to identify the role HR professionals *feel* they should be playing in acquisition planning and integration. Perhaps more importantly, the questions were designed to enable comparative assessments: respondents' attitudinal views on their ideal role versus the responses to questions posed on their actual, current role in the M&A process.

Rate the importance you place on HR's involvement in the following M&A activity:

Working With Management to Support Acquisition Strategy

Issue

The key to HR playing an increasingly substantive role in the M&A process is its involvement in the earliest stages, when corporate acquisition strategy is being articulated.

Findings

On a scale basis, the average response was 4.4.

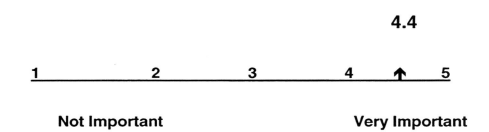

4.4

1   2   3   4 ↑ 5

Not Important   **Very Important**

> *"Only HR can ensure that a strategic and synergistic match exists and that the forward-looking business strategies of the acquisition can be successfully aligned."*
>
> **Corporate VP, Human Resources**
> **Software development company**

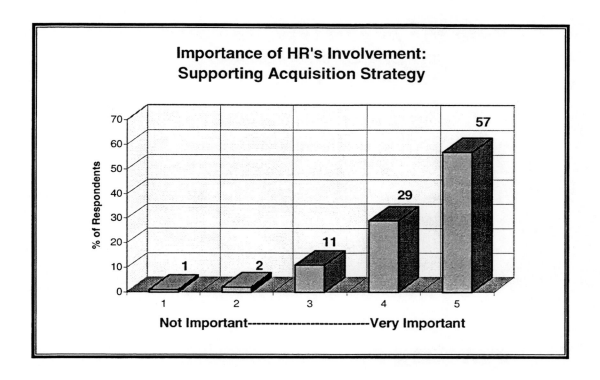

Importance of HR's Involvement: Supporting Acquisition Strategy

% of Respondents

Not Important---------------------------Very Important

Observations

From a percentage standpoint, 43% of those surveyed currently work with management to support acquisition strategy – but 86% (57% plus 29%), in this question, feel it is either *important* or *very important* to be doing so. Thus, there is a disconnect between the strategic role HR professionals are playing and that which they desire to play: virtually twice as many HR professionals *want* to be more involved in the strategic stages of M&A than actually are. The respondents rightfully believe that having acquisition strategy firmly grounded in a people-focused approach ensures that issues such as culture clashes and integration imperatives are addressed at the earliest point possible.

Rate the importance you place on HR's involvement in the following M&A activity:

Evaluating Target Companies/Screening Candidates

Issue

Senior management often relies on a small group of individuals to help assess acquisition targets. Input from strategic, financial, and operations managers acts as the primary screening criteria. But to what extent do HR professionals feel they should be part of the evaluative process?

Findings

On a scale basis, the average response was 3.4.

3.4

Not Important   **Very Important**

> *"HR must be directly involved – from the target (evaluation) stage, through post-merger performance review. HR should be an active member to drive all M&A activities, including but not limited to due diligence."*
>
> **VP, Human Resources**
> **Energy utility**

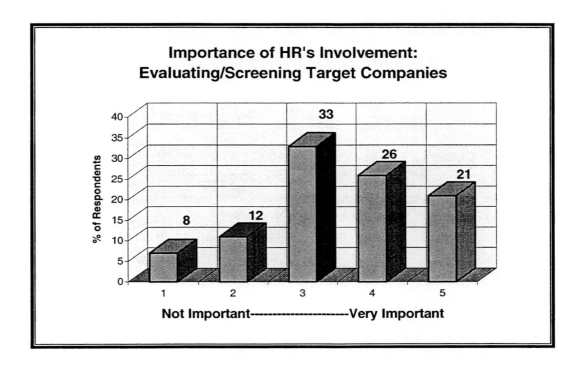

Importance of HR's Involvement: Evaluating/Screening Target Companies

% of Respondents

Not Important---------------------Very Important

Observations

Respondents evidently do not feel strongly that evaluating target companies is an important HR function. This is apparent from the scale average, as well as from a percentage standpoint, where a minority of the respondents (47%) felt that HR's involvement in evaluating target companies/screening candidates was either *important* or *very important*. The respondents' feelings mirror their current responsibilities: in an earlier question, only 34% reported participating in the process. HR, however, *should* be more involved. Earlier involvement would help to identify cultural mismatches and other readily apparent differences in work practices – HR issues that might prompt management to immediately forego negotiations with an ill-suited merger mate.

Rate the importance you place on HR's involvement in the following M&A activity:

Working on the Due Diligence Team

Issue

HR has made great strides in entering the previously private, historically finance-oriented world of due diligence. Indeed, an entire discipline known as HR due diligence is evolving.

Findings

On a scale basis, the average response was 4.6.

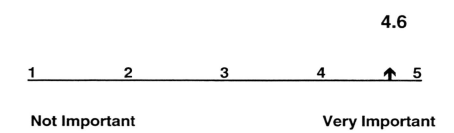

4.6

1   2   3   4   ↑ 5

Not Important   **Very Important**

"I believe HR's role should begin even prior to the due diligence process so management can have a more thorough understanding of the target company as a whole."

Director of Human Resources
Industrial products manufacturer

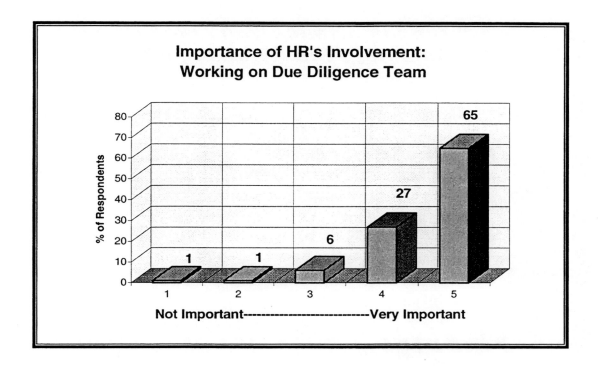

**Importance of HR's Involvement:
Working on Due Diligence Team**

% of Respondents

Not Important---------------------------Very Important

Observations

The survey findings indicate that working on due diligence represents HR's first entry into the M&A process. As cited earlier, 83% of respondents are involved in due diligence. In this question, more than 92% rated working on due diligence as either *important* or *very important*. There is an inconsistency, however, between the importance placed on due diligence and the lower level of importance placed on target company screening. In the one-on-one interviews conducted, an answer was provided: many respondents felt their lack of understanding of the overall acquisition process did not qualify them to participate in target company evaluations.

Rate the importance you place on HR's involvement in the following M&A activity:

Planning Post-Merger Integration

Issue

The survey sought to gauge the extent to which HR professionals feel they should be the planners of post-merger integration, as well as the tactical implementers of the various programs and activities involved. This particular question was designed to solicit feedback on the planning aspects of integration.

Findings

On a scale basis, the average response was 4.72.

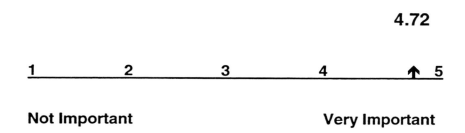

4.72

| 1 | 2 | 3 | 4 | ↑ 5 |

Not Important   **Very Important**

"Simply put, HR must assist senior management in the entire integration process – not just the implementation, but the planning as well."

VP, Human Resources
Pharmaceuticals manufacturer

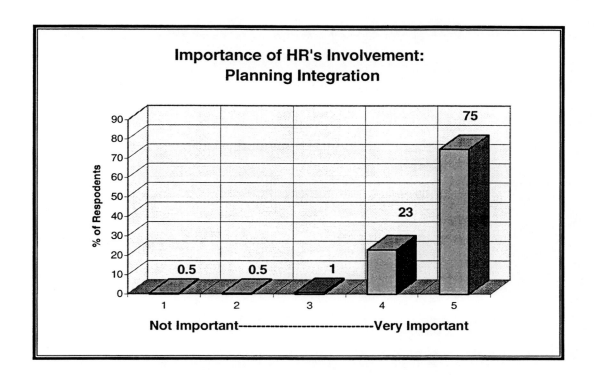

**Importance of HR's Involvement:
Planning Integration**

% of Respodents

Not Important-----------------------------Very Important

Observations

Clearly, HR professionals feel planning post-merger integration is their bailiwick. From a percentage standpoint, 23% of all respondents rated planning post–merger integration *important* and 75% rated this activity *very important* – totaling 98% of all responses. Based on the statistics and interviews, HR professionals see a direct connection between HR due diligence and integration planning ... and rightfully so. Many integration challenges and critical success factors come to light in the HR due diligence phase.

Rate the importance you place on HR's involvement in the following M&A activity:

Implementing Post-Merger Integration

Issue

Within the context of integration, there is a big difference between planning and implementation. The study strove to determine how important HR professionals felt their role was in the tactical implementation of integration initiatives.

Findings

On a scale basis, the average response was 4.73.

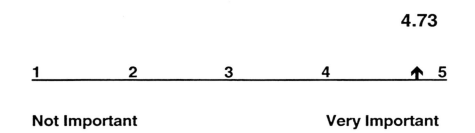

4.73

1   2   3   4   ↑ 5

Not Important   **Very Important**

"HR must be a 'full partner' with management in evaluating potential target companies all the way through implementing post-merger integration."

VP, Human Resources

International real estate/construction firm

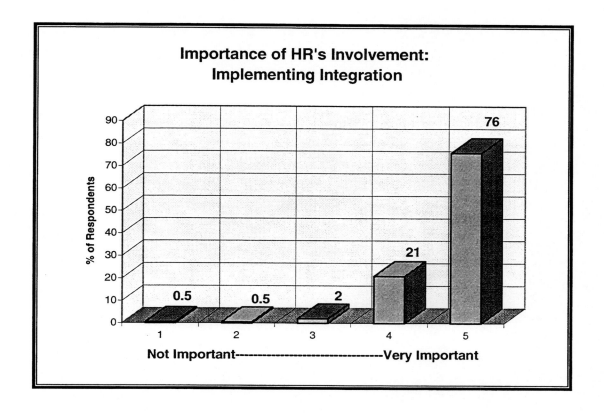

Importance of HR's Involvement: Implementing Integration

% of Respondents

Not Important--------------------------------Very Important

Observations

Unquestionably, respondents feel HR must not only plan integration but also must be directly involved in many aspects of its implementation. Seventy-six percent (76%) of all respondents viewed HR's involvement in implementing post-merger integration as *very important.* Another 21% viewed it as *important* – bringing the total of those who find this activity important in some way to 97%. In integration, HR must coordinate the melding of benefits and compensation plans, human resource information systems (HRIS), and assist management in devising the merged company's organizational structure. The attendant employee communications and training and development challenges related to these activities are obvious.

NOTES

Future Role of HR in Acquisition Planning and Integration

*H*aving elicited feedback regarding the current involvement of HR and the importance HR professionals place on specific M&A activities, the study posed questions regarding the role HR professionals feel they *ought to* be playing in the M&A process.

Some of the findings in this section indicated that HR is not involved in certain activities, yet respondents felt the function should play a more prominent role in them. It is apparent that HR continues to be more involved in acquisition planning and integration. Yet respondents feel they can be making an even more substantive strategic contribution.

However, a startling conclusion can be drawn from the findings: the vast majority of HR professionals do not feel they have sufficient technical knowledge to support the entire M&A process.

The respondents indicated the specific areas in which they would like to receive M&A-related training. The bottom line is that HR professionals feel they do not have the expertise to play a more comprehensive role, but desire continuing education to heighten their contribution to their companies' M&A programs.

Indicate your attitude toward the following statement:

HR Should Work With Management to Support Acquisition Strategy

Issue

Human resources has made some inroads as a strategic contributor to M&A. Still, less than half of those surveyed are actually involved in acquisition strategy development. The survey asked HR professionals if, in fact, they feel they should work with management in this phase of the M&A process.

Findings

On a scale basis, the average response was 4.6.

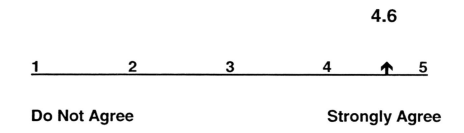

4.6

| 1 | 2 | 3 | 4 | ↑ 5 |

Do Not Agree   **Strongly Agree**

> *"HR should be involved very early in the acquisition process ... and must be seen as an equal player to all other functions (finance, operations, marketing)."*
>
> **VP, Human Resources**
> **Telecommunications company**

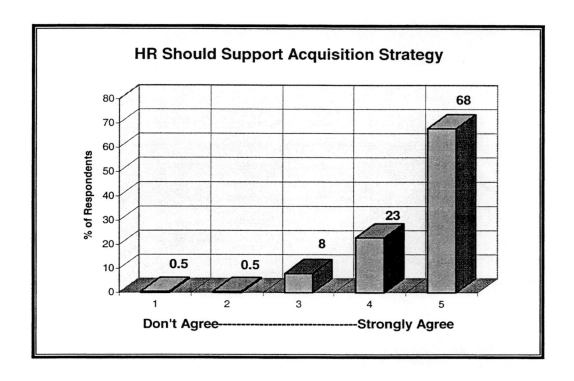

HR Should Support Acquisition Strategy

% of Respondents

Don't Agree-------------------------------Strongly Agree

Observations

Almost 91% of those surveyed agreed that HR should work with management to support acquisition strategy. This is in stark contrast to the 43% who currently are involved in that activity. Stated another way, less than half of all respondents actually work with management to support acquisition strategy – yet nine out of 10 respondents want to. In fact, 68% *strongly agree* (rank number 5) that HR should play a strategic role. Interestingly, the interviews revealed that most HR professionals lack an understanding of the causal links between human resource management and the strategic drivers of an M&A transaction. For instance, many respondents revealed widespread uncertainty about the connection of HR issues with a merged company's growth strategies.

Indicate your attitude toward the following statement:

HR Should Work with Management to Evaluate and Screen Target Companies

Issue

A logical extension of the strategy phase of acquisition planning is the evaluation and screening of target companies. The study sought HR professionals' thoughts on the importance of their future participation in the candidate evaluation process.

Findings

On a scale basis, the average response was 3.7.

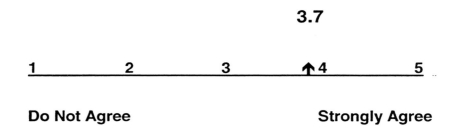

3.7

1   2   3   ↑4   5

Do Not Agree   **Strongly Agree**

> *"HR serves as the 'corporate conscience' on the M&A team."*
> **Senior VP, Human Resources**
> **Global insurance company**

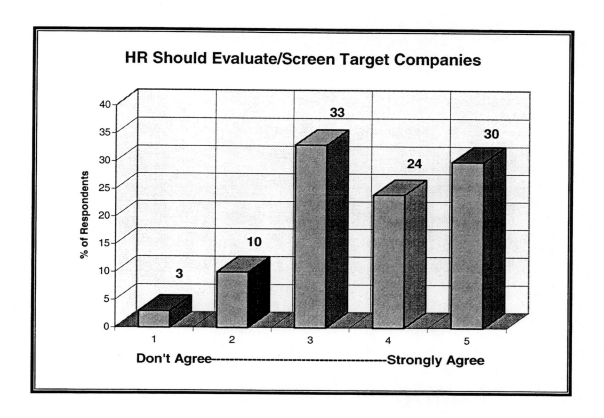

HR Should Evaluate/Screen Target Companies

% of Respondents

Don't Agree--Strongly Agree

Observations

Most respondents felt their involvement in target screening is important. From a percentage standpoint, only 13% did not agree that HR should play a role. However, almost one-third of the respondents were undecided. This left only a slight majority (54%) agreeing or strongly agreeing that HR should work in this capacity. The collective results of the study clearly indicate that respondents believe human resource issues must be investigated prior to an acquisition. In actuality, doing so should begin even before formal HR due diligence. Management's "short list" of acquisition candidates must be assessed from an HR standpoint as much as it is practicable. This is necessary to save the time, money and effort pursuing a candidate that never should have been courted in the first place because of fundamental personnel shortcomings or cultural compatibility issues.

Indicate your attitude toward the following statement:

HR-Related Issues Must Be Investigated Prior to the Start of Acquisition Negotiations

Issue

Even as its role expands in acquisition planning, HR's involvement is still largely relegated to activities in the tactical phases of the process. The criticality of people issues, however, may necessitate HR's participation in managerial investigations that occur *before* a target company has been approached and acquisition negotiations commence.

Findings

On a scale basis, the average response was 4.7.

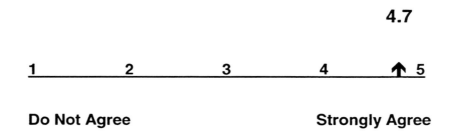

4.7

1   2   3   4   ↑ 5

Do Not Agree   Strongly Agree

"The success or failure of a merger or acquisition, more often than not, is governed by HR issues. HR should have a 'seat at the table' in all M&A activities and should be a key player throughout the process."

VP, Human Resources
Electronics manufacturer

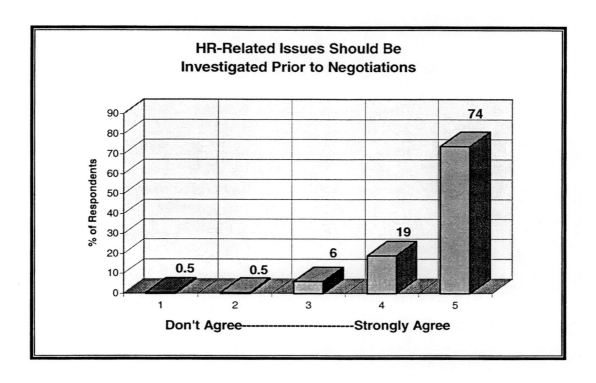

HR-Related Issues Should Be Investigated Prior to Negotiations

% of Respondents

0.5   0.5   6   19   74

Don't Agree-----------------------Strongly Agree

Observations

From a percentage standpoint, nearly all respondents (93%) either *agree* (19%) or *strongly agree* (74%) that HR-related issues must be investigated prior to the start of formal acquisition negotiations. The findings represent an overwhelming affirmation of the respondents' belief that HR issues must pervade pre-deal planning activities. The findings also highlight the disparity between what HR professionals are assigned in pre-merger activities and what they feel they ought to be assigned – as the earlier questions citing their low level of involvement in "acquisition strategy development" and "target company screening" indicate.

Indicate your attitude toward the following statement:

Most HR Professionals Have Sufficient Technical Knowledge of M&A and Other Corporate Growth Activities to Support Acquisition Strategy Development

Issue

All told, the survey findings confirmed three issues: 1) HR professionals believe their involvement in acquisition planning and integration is important; 2) they are more broadly involved in the process than ever before; and 3) they feel they can and should be more involved than they are now. Yet M&A is an extremely complex process that requires distinct technical knowledge gained through real-life experience or, at least, simulative preparation. This question asked respondents to assess their technical knowledge of the M&A process in order to make a greater strategic contribution to their companies' acquisition-oriented corporate growth activities.

Findings

On a scale basis, the average response was 2.7.

2.7

| 1 | 2 | ↑ 3 | 4 | 5 |

Do Not Agree   **Strongly Agree**

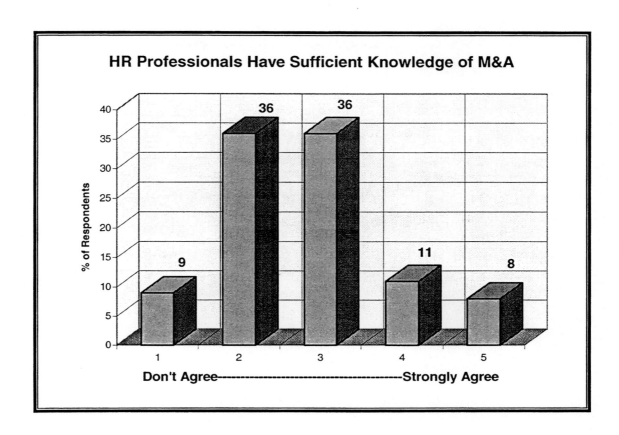

HR Professionals Have Sufficient Knowledge of M&A

Don't Agree--Strongly Agree

Observations

Only 19% (11% and 8%) of respondents believe that most HR professionals have sufficient technical knowledge of the M&A process to support acquisition strategy development. *More than 80% were unsure or felt they lack the critical knowledge.* Indeed, this lack of knowledge and experience is ostensibly the reason why HR is not being brought in by senior management to directly support acquisition strategy and target company evaluations. HR professionals receive training in change-management, organizational design and leadership throughout their careers. At no point in this training are they getting the same level of guidance on M&A. This must change in light of the increasing prevalence of M&A as a primary corporate growth strategy.

Indicate your attitude toward the following statement:

HR Professionals Can Benefit From Technical Training to Support Acquisition Strategy Development and Target Company Evaluation/Screening

Issue

Given their actual and desired role in M&A, the study solicited HR professionals' views on the benefit of specialized training in this area.

Findings

On scale basis, the average response was 4.2.

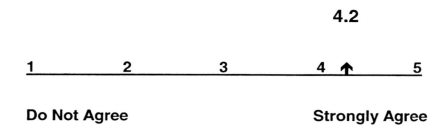

4.2

| 1 | 2 | 3 | 4 ↑ | 5 |

Do Not Agree   Strongly Agree

> "HR is key to the M&A process. But many HR professionals are typically unprepared to handle the responsibilities that come with the territory if they don't have the prior experience."
> **Senior VP, Human Resources**
> **Chemicals manufacturer**

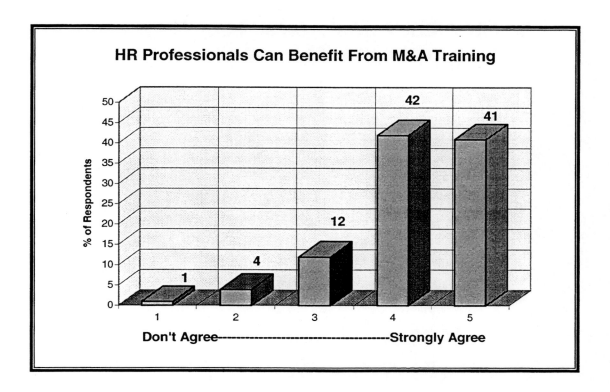

HR Professionals Can Benefit From M&A Training

Don't Agree---------------------------------------Strongly Agree

Observations

HR professionals obviously recognize the value of training to effect personal and professional growth. In this study, they recognize the need for their own training in the complex business process that is M&A. Forty-two percent (42%) of all respondents *agree* and 41% *strongly agree* that HR professionals can benefit from technical training (combined, the responses total 83% of respondents indicating overall agreement). Thus, respondents overwhelmingly recognize that they do not have enough technical knowledge to support the more strategic aspects of acquisition planning. For HR professionals to advance to the next level, they must receive technical training. Their need is apparent. So too is their desire.

What M&A training will help HR professionals play a more valuable role in the process?

Issue

The study asked respondents to indicate in what specific M&A-related area(s) they require continuing education.

Findings

The number-one area of training sought by HR professionals was *due diligence*, with 80% of respondents citing the need. Seventy-five percent (75%) require training in the *acquisition process*; 58% need guidance in M&A-specific *employee communications*; 57% require training in *strategic planning*. *Organizational behavior* rounded out the top five requested areas of training (51%). Other areas, such as *corporate finance,* and *assessment and selection*, garnered approximately one-third of respondents' votes, while marketing yielded a scant 11%.

"Besides financial considerations, most M&A projects fail on the people side. Success means getting it right early. The 'deal makers' should have HR professionals 'at the table' who understand the link between people and growth strategies like M&A."

VP, Human Resources
Air travel company

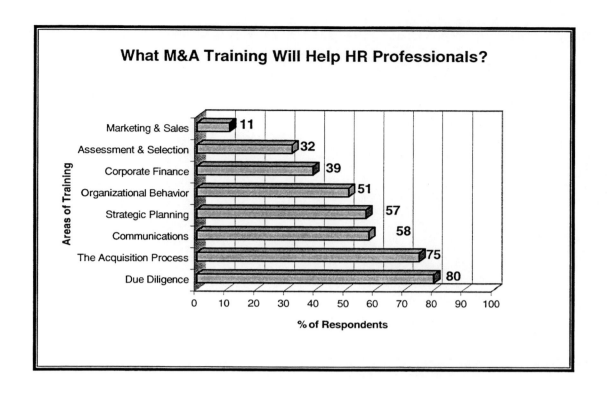

What M&A Training Will Help HR Professionals?

Areas of Training	% of Respondents
Marketing & Sales	11
Assessment & Selection	32
Corporate Finance	39
Organizational Behavior	51
Strategic Planning	57
Communications	58
The Acquisition Process	75
Due Diligence	80

Observations

M&A-specific training is rarely part of HR professionals' education. Yet, more and more, they are being called upon by management to contribute in diverse ways to their companies' merger and acquisition activities. To make an increasingly valuable contribution, HR must intimately understand the entire acquisition process – from a multi-disciplinary perspective. For instance, virtually the same number of respondents who said they were involved in performing due diligence, (83%), also said they requested technical training in that area (80%). This reveals their desire to have a comprehensive understanding of the entire process. The important role that HR professionals play in corporate combinations is being increasingly endorsed by senior management. To be sure, HR is on the front lines of M&A today. Once HR is able to contribute more broadly to the strategic and tactical battle plan, companies will directly increase their chances of winning at mergers and acquisitions.

NOTES

M&A Skills Development for Human Resource Professionals

Survey respondents indicated the desire to receive training in the mechanics of merger and acquisition planning and integration. They specifically cited the need for guidance in the following areas:

➢ Acquisition process (including strategy development)

➢ Due diligence

➢ Employee communications

➢ (M&A-influenced) organizational behavior

Respondents indicated less interest in the need for training in several other areas, which, in actuality, are central to ensuring success in corporate mergers and acquisitions. The following areas fall either directly or indirectly under HR's purview. Going forward, however, HR professionals must broaden their understanding of the role they play in supporting:

➢ Employee sensing and research

➢ Assessment and selection

➢ Training and development

➢ Marketing and sales

In this section, high-level guidance is provided on each of these aspects of acquisition planning and integration.

HR professionals in larger organizations are taking an increasingly broader role in the M&A process and are gaining the necessary experience. What's more, many acquisitive companies are adopting uniform processes to standardize and refine their acquisition planning and integration activities. The following guidance is designed to help the great majority of HR professionals who do not work in such organizations or who have not yet gained extensive experience in the various aspects of M&A.

The Acquisition Process

*H*R professionals can make a broader contribution to their companies' M&A activities by more fully understanding the acquisition process.

Within the context of pre-deal planning, there are three discrete activities to which HR should contribute. The role of HR in each area varies on a company-by-company basis. Following is a description of each phase:

1. M&A strategy development/strategic planning

2. Target company identification and screening

3. Integration planning

M&A Strategy Development/Strategic Planning

Companies undertake mergers and acquisitions to effect corporate growth. Growth is sought through various *strategic drivers*: attaining new products and services; penetrating new markets; gaining access to new distribution channels; and acquiring emerging technologies (to aid in product development, manufacturing, or to bolster ties with customers and other stakeholders). Increasingly, a main goal of M&A is acquiring human or intellectual assets (e.g., key knowledge workers). HR plays its greatest and most significant role when this is the case.

In many respects, M&A strategy development mirrors the corporate strategic planning process. Devising M&A strategy requires that a company:

➤ Assess its current standing in the marketplace relative to competitors

➤ Ascertain current and future customer needs

➤ Identify its corporate growth needs and objectives (those that will drive value)

➤ Evaluate companies whose acquired capabilities can help the merged firm accomplish those goals

HR's Role in M&A Strategy Development

Today, most mergers and acquisitions are done to strengthen a company's competitive standing. Typically, the acquiring firm seeks *growth synergies* tied to the aforementioned strategic drivers. Other times, the company seeks *cost-reduction synergies* that are based on lowering operating expenses by eliminating duplicative people, products and processes and achieving economies of scale. Often, both approaches are combined. Yet each approach poses different challenges and roles for HR professionals:

➤ **Cost-reduction synergies are sought**

In the wake of a merger or acquisition, the largest area of cutbacks is typically in the personnel arena. HR's involvement is critical in helping to support cost/benefit analyses on the number of staff to be terminated, how those cutbacks will impact the combined company's operational infrastructure, and the financial ramifications of benefit and severance packages and employee out-placement programs (to name just a few financial issues relative to personnel decision-making). HR should also play a role in coordinating post-merger assessment and selection, when guidance on determining the requisite skill sets is needed to drive decisions on how many and who to cut. (See page 146.)

➤ **Revenue growth synergies are sought**

This is the more common goal of M&A today – driving long-term revenues. HR must work closely with management to realize the growth synergies sought. Specifically, HR must

---

spearhead the process of identifying key human assets in the target company, advising on the retention of those key employees, and supporting the physical deployment of employees in selected markets and product areas. Additionally, HR must focus on developing reward and recognition and training and development programs to foster teamwork, motivate the rank and file, and facilitate post-merger integration. (See page 150.)

Target Company Identification and Screening

Upon determining the company's strategic goals, management then tries to identify a partner who can help the company attain them. In some instances, management observes a particular capability resident in another company. Simply envisioning that capability merged with the acquirer can trigger an acquisition strategy. Other times, an investment banker will bring acquisition candidates to management's attention. Larger firms have in-house corporate development professionals who perform this and other transactional duties.

Eventually, management will contact the target company to express interest in a possible corporate combination. Then a "letter of intent" or "offer letter" is presented, which begins the negotiation process between the two firms. The due diligence process follows in which managements of both firms engage in a detailed analysis of each other's finances and operations. (Information on the due diligence process, and HR's specific responsibilities, appears in the next section.) Ultimately, this phase culminates with a definitive agreement to consummate the transaction.

HR's role in target company identification and screening

HR contributes the all-important *people* perspective to this phase of the process. HR assesses such crucial variables as marketplace perceptions of a given company's employee base, and broad organizational differences that may exist in the would-be merger partners' collective belief systems and attitudes. At this stage of the process, HR's primary contributions are determining whether a target company offers the quality human assets sought, and assessing the "integratability" of the target's employees with those of the acquiring firm. Corporate culture is one important part of HR's initial assessment. Yet this and a myriad of other HR and benefits-related issues are examined in detail in the due diligence process.

Integration Planning

Too many companies leave integration planning until after the close of the transaction. This has proven to be a mistake. Integration planning should begin immediately after the "offer letter" has been signed and the due diligence process commences.

HR's role in integration planning

Integration is a broad and complex undertaking that can last anywhere from months to years, depending on the size of the transaction and numerous other organizational variables (e.g., the extent to which the combining companies are culturally dissimilar or geographically dispersed). The primary roles of HR in integration planning are devising employee retention strategies, developing employee communication programs and aligning benefits and compensation processes. HR must also focus on strategic staffing – a significant determinant in cultivating the merged firm's requisite skill base. Integration planning also requires HR to swiftly assess employee needs and design corresponding training and development initiatives (see page 150.)

Note: It is imperative that HR work closely with other corporate functions during integration planning to factor staffing issues into all aspects of operational decision-making.

Due Diligence

*D*ue diligence is the detailed examination of a target company's finances and operations undertaken prior to finalization of a merger or acquisition.

Due diligence has a two-fold purpose. First, it is used as a valuation tool to determine the most accurate value of a target company's assets – tangible and intangible. Second, due diligence is the most direct method for spotting liabilities in the areas of accounting, tax, operations, marketing and human resources. The results of each of these investigations are used to help the acquiring company arrive at the target's purchase price.

Attorneys, accountants, tax advisors, and operations specialists have historically comprised the due diligence team. However, as the rate of M&A deal failures has skyrocketed, management has begun broadening the due diligence team to include professionals from other functional areas. HR is one function that has traditionally been excluded from the due diligence process, but which is now playing a more substantive role (as the results of this study clearly show).

Following are descriptions of the main investigative areas of due diligence and the primary focus of each:

➢ Accounting

➢ Tax

➢ Legal and regulatory

➢ Operational

➢ Marketing

➢ Human resources

Accounting

The role of accountants on the due diligence team is evaluating a merger partner's historical financial performance. This includes conducting a detailed review of financial statements. Additionally, accounting due diligence keys on identifying undervalued, over-valued or unrecorded assets and liabilities. From an HR standpoint, this often includes valuations tied to qualified and non-qualified pension and deferred compensation obligations – including, but not limited to, retiree medical and executive severance plans.

Tax

Tax specialists are also involved the valuation of the M&A candidate, as well as advising the acquiring company on deal structuring relative to income tax and accounting considerations. Their primary focus is on assessing the merger partner's current situation in terms of its historical tax compliance and any existing or potential tax problems.

Legal and Regulatory

In public company transactions, due diligence involves the review of SEC filings such as Forms 8-K, 10-K, 10-Q and registration statements. The specialists coordinating regulatory due diligence ensure compliance with all SEC rules governing merger and acquisition activity. They are also responsible for drafting transaction-related contracts and agreements in accordance with various local, state and federal laws.

Operational

A key activity, operational due diligence involves assessing the target company's overall infrastructure, organizational systems and managerial processes. The focus is on understanding how the target company is structured, how it physically produces and distributes its goods and services, and how it runs on a day-to-day basis. Effective integration of the merged firm's operations is contingent upon a thorough understanding of the systems and processes, which can be first evaluated during due diligence.

Marketing

With the focus of strategic mergers on effecting long-term revenue-growth, this new area of analysis has emerged. Marketing due diligence assesses a target company's growth-related strengths and weaknesses to ensure the success of strategic mergers and acquisitions. Marketing due diligence transcends traditional due diligence by its dual nature – it focuses on both "defensive" (risk avoidance) and "offensive" (growth) aspects of a target company evaluation. From a defensive standpoint, it helps an acquirer avoid the delays, missteps, and financial losses that can result from inadequate examinations of the target and the markets in which it operates. From an offensive standpoint, marketing due diligence identifies, quantifies and prioritizes the revenue enhancement opportunities attainable by the merged company. (See page 154 for more information on post-merger revenue generation and HR's role in the process.)

Human Resources Due Diligence

An entire investigative area has evolved in the form of HR-specific due diligence. This is consistent with the increasing importance of the people-related aspects of acquisition planning and integration.

Cultural Compatibility
HR due diligence often begins with the process of identifying the cultural compatibility between combining companies. This analysis has as its key focus identifying the extent to which the merging

merging companies are similar or dissimilar in the defining characteristics of corporate culture.

By and large, the post-merger integration challenge is heightened when there are many areas of dissimilarity. (Indeed, some M&A transactions should proceed with great caution – or should be canceled outright – when a high degree of incompatibility is identified in the cultural analysis phase.) Integration is generally likely to proceed more smoothly when there are multiple areas of commonality.

Culture must be defined before it can be assessed. One way of defining culture is by assessing it in terms of *structural, political* and *emotional* variables:

> **Structural**

Culture is determined, in part, by structural factors that include, for example, the size, age and history of the company; the industry in which it operates; the geographic location of the company's operations; and whether it is a product or service provider. Typically, these are the non-dynamic issues that an acquired company brings to the mix. They should be studied because, collectively, they influence how a company works on a day-to-day basis and how its employees interact with each other, their customers, and their markets. Consider, for example, the structural variable of geography. Companies in different parts of the country tend to do business differently from firms in other areas – for instance, the so-called "laid back" West Coast firm versus the "hyper-aggressive" East Coast type. The fact remains that companies that serve a customer base in a given geographic area must craft their products, processes and operations to the buyers within those markets. It may be rightly assumed, therefore, that regional companies adopt the culture (or at least some of the salient traits) of the regional culture in which they compete. In an M&A context, regional cultural differences can lead to unusually high employee turnover rates within the merged firm.

➢ Political

From a political standpoint, culture is defined by the distribution of power throughout the organization and the primary modes of managerial decision-making. A company's political composition sets the tone within an organization that directly impacts employees' functional activities and contributes to the sentiments employees hold toward their roles within the company. Corporate cultures move along a continuum that modulates from a dictatorial point of reference on one extreme, to one of total employee empowerment on the other. Comparing where your company and your merger partner are plotted along this *cultural control continuum* offers important insights into the likelihood of cultural compatibility. The control continuum transcends issues of company size and exists within all firms regardless of their industry. Considering that the CEO is the starting point of all power in an organization, the first step is to determine the extent to which power is concentrated within that office – and, subsequently, how and where power is bestowed upon managers at lower levels of the hierarchy. Once ascertained, you will be able to find where the organization fits on the control continuum and determine how it compares to your own company's political personality. Merging organizations that are at opposite ends of the continuum have a higher likelihood of experiencing employee conflict and defections before an integration program is even implemented.

➢ Emotional

Culture is also influenced by the personal feelings individual employees hold toward the company, its policies, and the overall corporate context. On an emotional level, corporate culture is defined as the collective thoughts, habits, attitudes and patterns of behavior from *the employee's individual perspective*. When a person is hired into a given organization, he or she buys into a set of cultural guidelines – in essence, a "cultural contract" that dictates the employee's day-to-day activities and behavior. Management further establishes the framework of this culture by laying down the parameters of employee behavior. Over a period of time, the synthesis of personalities and environmental influences meld to become defining traits of the corporate culture. The building blocks of this shared belief system are the general attitudes and opinions that employees hold toward such things as:

- The leadership of the company
- Management's structure and style
- Level of autonomy granted to middle managers
- Level of commitment to one's superior, job and company
- Perceived fairness of total compensation
- Overall job satisfaction
- Other company-specific variables

CLEMENTE, GREENSPAN & CO., INC.

HR Due Diligence Checklist

The initial assessment of cultural compatibility is followed by a detailed analysis of the M&A candidate's HR systems and processes. Following is a list of the most important areas that must be examined in the investigative process:

- ❑ Organizational structure
- ❑ Human resources inventory (including skills, capabilities and experience)
- ❑ Compensation system
- ❑ Direct compensation programs (including base, differential, and incentive pay programs)
- ❑ Wage and salary issues
- ❑ Indirect compensation system
- ❑ Health & welfare plans
- ❑ Defined benefit/pension plans
- ❑ Defined contribution plans
- ❑ Defined contribution issues (including asset allocation options and corporate matching)
- ❑ Benefit plans for active personnel
- ❑ Retirement benefits – other than pension plans
- ❑ Outsourcing vendors and programs
- ❑ Insurance and disability vendors and programs
- ❑ Workers compensation
- ❑ Outside HR services (e.g., retained benefits consultants)
- ❑ Labor-related issues and labor agreements
- ❑ Labor-management relations
- ❑ Job descriptions and context

- [ ] Employment contracts
- [ ] Assessment process
- [ ] Selection process
- [ ] Hiring policies and procedures
- [ ] Performance appraisal policies and procedures
- [ ] Termination policies
- [ ] Severance policies
- [ ] Replacement plans
- [ ] Succession plans
- [ ] Incentive programs
- [ ] Perquisites
- [ ] Expense reimbursement policies and procedures
- [ ] Training and development programs
- [ ] Costs involved in integrating HR policies
- [ ] Costs involved in personnel relocations
- [ ] Diversity issues and policies
- [ ] Health, safety and security issues
- [ ] Human Resource Information Systems (HRIS) issues (including payroll systems)
- [ ] Expatriate employee issues
- [ ] Voice- and e-mail systems and other internal communication media

Employee Communications

A merger or acquisition represents a massive organizational change initiative that requires a very specific approach to designing and executing employee communication programs. To effectively contribute to an M&A communications program, HR professionals must understand:

1. Communication challenges posed by M&A

2. Audience analysis criteria

3. Communication content for various phases of the M&A process

Communication Challenges Posed by M&A

Employee uncertainty in evolving M&A transactions, coupled with the magnitude and fast pace of change, heighten the importance of quickly and efficiently implementing internal communication programs. HR professionals coordinating the communication process must focus on two key challenges: addressing employee fears, and communicating with new audiences.

➢ **Addressing employee fears**

Workers in *both* organizations are uncertain about their future roles in the merged company. Too often, managers think that it is only the people in the acquired company who experience M&A angst. Not true. Until final decisions have been made on significant organizational decisions and individual employees' fates, communications should emphasize the growth potential for all employees in the new company; the message must be sent that the transaction is designed to better and grow the organization – a fact that translates into advancement opportunities for many employees. Above all, *ensure that communications are truthful. If there is bad news to communicate (e.g., imminent layoffs, relocations) communicate it swiftly and tactfully.* Never lie or be evasive. If there are not specific details to report, say so ... but tell employees when specifics will be provided. In some instances, it may even be better to make uncomfortable announcements so that the workforce can continue to move forward and focus on the future.

➢ **Communicating with new audiences**

Recognize that employees from the acquired firm are used to receiving communications in certain ways, through certain media, and at certain frequencies. It is important to determine through what channels they have historically received internal communications (e.g., newsletters, e-mail, memoranda) and the frequency with which they have received them. Also take note of the tone of past communications. Were they formal, informal, serious, humorous, etc? The thing to keep in mind is that *effectively communicating with new audiences requires – at least initially – reaching them in the ways they are accustomed to being reached.*

Audience Analysis Criteria

A large part of devising effective communications is understanding the acquired company's employees. Audience analysis is necessary to shape messages to maximize their motivational and rhetorical impact.

One message will not suffice for all employees. For example, older employees will have very different concerns than those at the younger end of the workforce spectrum. As early as possible, HR must gauge the composition of the acquired company's employee base vis-a-vis three variables: demographics, geographics and psychographics (Note: "Cultural due diligence" should lend valuable insight into these areas):

Demographics

This includes data on the age, gender, education level, and socio-economic composition of the employee base. There, of course, may be a strong mix of employees with different demographic traits. But it is necessary to identify – by and large – the overall make-up of the employee base. For instance, is it generally young or old? Is it highly educated (at the managerial ranks) or more blue-collar?

Geographics

If the target is a regional firm, will the acquiring employees mesh with the make-up of the geographic locale (for instance, a conservative Midwest-based company being acquired by a progressive Southern California one)? Obviously, avoid stereotyping. But recognize that many times a company's employees will adopt some of the broader sociological and attitudinal traits of the geographic locales in which they operate.

Psychographics

This refers to the employee base's collective attitudes toward their jobs. Psychographics relate to the personal feelings individual employees hold toward the company, its policies, and the overall corporate context. You must understand employees' attitudes toward such areas as the leadership of the company; management's structure and style; level of commitment to one's superior, job and company; perceived fairness of total compensation. Weakened morale and productivity problems can quickly arise when employees used to being closely monitored are acquired by an entrepreneurial company that advocates self-motivation.

Communication Content for Various Phases of the M&A Process

Different phases of the M&A process involve different communication objectives. These tie directly to the aforementioned challenges (e.g., allaying employee fears) and to employees' overriding need and desire for information.

> ## Phase One (deal announcement)

In this phase, basic information must be imparted. Communications take the form of the so-called "5 W's of journalistic reportage": The merger or acquisition is taking place (the "what"); background on the company being acquired or merged with (the "who"); the timing of the transaction's closing (the "when"); the strategic intent of the deal ("why"); and, where appropriate, the location of the merger partner relative to the markets in which it operates (the "where").

> ## Phase Two (deal closing and 1-3 months after closing)

Information disseminated in this phase must focus on the expected impact the transaction will have on the combined firm's employee base. Specific information must be imparted; *this is not the time for communication generalities.* HR professionals must be prepared to focus on whether or not there will be layoffs; benefits and health insurance program changes (including, for example, how the merger will affect accrued pension benefits); managerial appointments; anticipated employee relocations; changes in performance reviews and salary increases; personal time-off and sick pay policies; etc. At this critical stage of the merger or acquisition, managerial and leadership appointments must be announced. Communicating these decisions early in the process will go a long way toward retaining and motivating key employees, whose positive responses will influence others.

> ### Phase Three (integration implementation; 1-6 months after closing)

All subsequent communications must directly support integration activities. The primary goals of post–merger communications are to inform and, more importantly, to inspire. Communications must convey compelling reasons why the merged firm is now a better place to work. Communications must achieve buy–in and, in doing so, build strong commitment to the merged firm's strategic vision. The specific activities being undertaken to integrate the merging companies must be communicated to employees. Progress and successes being achieved by individual departments and employees must be chronicled and widely disseminated.

Critical Success Factors

1. Communicate early and often throughout all stages of the evolving M&A process

2. Understand the new audiences you will be communicating with (including the channels through which they are used to receiving information)

3. Devise communications to directly support the integration process, widely chronicling progress and successes being attained

4. Be as specific and truthful as possible

5. Make sure your messages are consistent

6. When uncertain, always over-communicate rather than risk under-communicating

7. Leverage communications into an internal recruiting tool

8. Focus on the future

9. Don't promise what can't be delivered; disappointments compound their negative affect

10. Keep the flow of information two-way; ask for feedback

Organizational Behavior

*E*mployee attitudes and actions take on markedly distinct characteristics in the context of a merger or acquisition. Any employee who has lived through a major M&A event knows how differently employees think and act after the transaction is announced and, subsequently, when it is finalized.

HR professionals must recognize the common sentiments and feelings employees experience. This is critical in order to protect and cultivate the merged company's human assets — and it is the key to managing and accelerating the organizational change process. HR professionals must understand:

➤ Employee psychology

➤ Employee behaviors

➤ Coping with M&A-influenced organizational behavior

Employee Psychology

Many employees involved in a merger or acquisition tend to exhibit the following traits:

➤ **Uncertainty**

Employees at all levels of the organization experience, to some degree, uncertainty about their future. Often, rampant insecurity results from people's questions about whether or not they will have jobs upon the transaction's close; will their current staff level change; will their job responsibilities or reporting relationships change; etc. Unfortunately, in the early stages of an M&A transaction, there is typically a lack of information to assuage employees' fears, since staffing and organizational decisions have yet to be finalized

➤ **Fear/distrust**

The lack of information fosters fear. Employees expect the worst to happen (e.g., that they will lose their jobs, be asked to re-locate, accept demotions in rank or compensation). Fear breeds distrust, particularly of managers and employees from the "other side." Distrust may also arise between workers from the same organization. One-time teammates may indeed be leery about possibly losing their job to a co-worker.

➤ **Anger and resentment**

There are almost always people displeased with the final outcome of post-merger staffing and organizational decisions. Anger and resentment, obviously, are common amongst employees being terminated. But such emotions also arise amongst the ranks of employees who have been spared if, for example, many of their friends and co-workers have not been. Personnel decisions are just one source of employee angst. Other issues, such as re-assignments and shifts in policies and procedures, may spawn additional hostility.

Employee Behaviors

The psychological climate engenders distinct behaviors and patterns of employee interaction:

➤ **Lack of productivity and personal initiative**

Employee productivity will drop precipitously prior to the finalization of major staffing and organizational decisions. Work hours will be taken up with co-workers speculating about their future prospects. The dearth of details will prompt employees to spend inordinate amounts of time seeking out information from co-workers and other sources. People concerned about their positions will fear making mistakes, lest the new management seize on errors as cause for terminations. Aggressive, highly motivated employees' will cease taking chances — again for fear of making mistakes that may violate the new management's policies and procedures.

➤ Spread of misinformation

When there is no information, employees create it. When there is little information, employees are left to fill in the gaps. The result is rumors and mis-information disseminated across all levels of the organization. Employee fear and uncertainty leads to worst-case-scenario speculation. The grapevine is filled with bits and pieces of information on the negative fate of people and programs. Usually, there is little truth in many of these prognostications. But misinformation is powerful in its ability to shape negative employee attitudes and spark widespread organizational pessimism.

➤ Protecting one's turf

Many employees necessarily become protective of their positions. Teamwork all but disappears as current projects stall. Two basic types of behavior will arise: Some people will seek to impress the new management team by aggressively presenting their capabilities and accomplishments; they will strive to draw attention to their past achievements and future potential. The more passive employees will try to *avoid* bringing attention to themselves. They will continue to work quietly without drawing the notice of new managers. Their efforts to fortify their standing will be much more subtle. But the intention of safeguarding their position is the same as their more aggressive counterparts. The result in both instances is negative synergy. Ideas are jealously guarded and innovation is quashed as employees attempt to insulate themselves.

Coping With M&A-Influenced Organizational Behavior

Through carefully tailored communications and training and development programs, organizational behavior can be positively influenced. All such activities should focus on the following:

> **Helping employees deal with the inevitability of change**

Things rarely remain the same in the wake of a major transaction. Roles and responsibilities change. People often are terminated or re-assigned. New policies and procedures are adopted. Employees must be aided, and psychologically prepared, to accept the changes that are inevitable. They must also be made to understand that additional changes may have to be enacted in the future as the integration process moves through its various stages. Helping employees to accept and understand change will accelerate the process and minimize the pain associated with uncertainty.

> **Highlighting opportunities for employees' personal/professional growth**

As stated, most mergers today are designed to make the combining firms more powerful than they were as independent companies. This fact points up opportunities for the professional prospects of employees at all levels of the new company. The possibilities for personal growth, advancement and financial remuneration must be key messages in all post-merger communication and training programs. Such motivational information is critical to effect maximum productivity of individuals and teams.

> **Detailing ways employees can directly support (and be rewarded for) corporate growth**

Employees that are personally involved in corporate growth will be more committed to attaining that growth. It is important to carve out specific responsibilities for employees in growth programs such as integration teams and work groups. People's responsibilities – along with their attendant goals and rewards – should be clear and measurable. The adage "A rising tide lifts all boats" is a theme that should be sounded often and widely to foster individual employees' commitment and motivation.

Employee Sensing and Research

Implementing communication and training and development programs to facilitate post-merger integration requires gauging employees' attitudes and sentiments at regular intervals in the post-transaction timetable. A combination of focus groups, surveys, and questionnaire research should be designed to gain insights on:

1. Employees' attitudes toward the merger or acquisition

2. Information needed by employees

3. Organizational requirements for ongoing cultural alignment

Employees' Attitudes Toward the Merger or Acquisition

Assessing employees' sentiments toward the merger or acquisition is central to tailoring communications and change-management initiatives to foster unity, teamwork and collegiality. Lapses in productivity are common in this early stage of integration. In a 2,000-employee organization, where one half of the workforce is spending an hour each day discussing the uncertainties of the merger, a newly merged company can lose 1,000 hours per day in productivity. Assuming an average wage of $50 per hour, this wasted time can deliver a weekly loss to the bottom line of $250,000 per week! HR's efforts can make a critical cost-saving contribution. Specially designed attitude surveys should be devised — one to three months after close of the transaction — to generate employee feedback on the following key areas:

➤ **Integration progress**

Do employees feel integration is proceeding smoothly? If not, why? Can they recommend ways to expedite or facilitate the process? Are efforts being made to mitigate the "us vs. them" mentality?

> **Emotional issues**

If there have been layoffs, for example, do the employees who have been maintained feel confident in their current standing and future prospects? How do they feel about the fact that there were layoffs (e.g., do they harbor resentment toward management)? Are remaining employees more likely to follow their key influencers out the door, or have they been given compelling reasons to stay?

> **Equality**

Do they feel there has been an equal distribution of responsibility granted to managers from both of the merging companies? Do they feel there has been inequality in which one firm's employees got the "plum" assignments or territories? Do acquired employees feel like second-class citizens? In general, do they feel both sets of employees are being treated fairly?

Information Needed by Employees (first month after closing)

Post-merger productivity can only be effected when employees understand important administrative and operational procedures – as well as core issues relative to the merged company's strategic goals and objectives. HR must research whether or not employees are aware of the following critical issues:

> **Job requirements and performance**

Do employees understand what will be expected of them in terms of specific new job responsibilities, as well as how they will be evaluated? Do they understand what criteria will be used in the appraisal process, and when promotions and salary increases will be granted?

➤ General organization and administration

Do employees know how the merged firm is structured, who the key executives are, and how the lines of reporting are set up? Do they understand how the merged company runs on a day-to-day basis (e.g., in terms of purchasing procedures, time and expense reporting)?

➤ Benefits

Do employees fully understand their new benefits and the provisions of the company's health and welfare programs? Do they know how to file health insurance claims? Do they fully understand the particulars of the company's retirement plans?

➤ Mission and values

Do employees understand the *reason* for the transaction and the strategic direction of the merged company – including how it is positioned in the marketplace vis-a-vis competitors? Do they understand what customer-service or -relations roles employees play at different levels of the organization?

➤ Products and services

Do they know the full range of offerings of the combined firm? Do they understand the company's products' competitive differentiators? Have they been trained in the benefits to the customer of buying these products from the newly merged firm? Often relegated to a lower training priority, educating both acquired and acquiring employees on the combined company's breadth of products and/or services creates a common platform on which employees can share information. Additionally, it is critical that those on the front lines in customer-contact positions – sales, service, and support – are well-versed in the specifics of the new company's complete product and service lines and are presenting a uniform picture of the company.

Receiving immediate feedback on these core issues will help HR identify employee deficiencies and, thus, develop appropriate content for orientation and training programs.

Organizational Requirements for Ongoing Cultural Alignment (3-6 months after closing)

The findings from research on prevailing attitudes and informational gaps can be applied to devising training and development programs in different administrative and operational areas. Both formal and informal research should also lend insight into the training that will take place over a longer time period to support ongoing cultural alignment. This research should focus on:

➤ **Communication content and channels**

What have been the most effective messages and media for reaching the merged company's employees? (Initial attempts at disseminating internal communications may need to be modified to facilitate cultural alignment.)

➤ **Communication sources**

Who have been the most influential sources (e.g., certain managers) in communicating details of the merger and the integration program? Have "opinion leaders" or key influencers evolved? (If so, these people should play a greater communications role going forward.) Have negative communication sources surfaced? Are there individuals who have publicly refused to adapt to the new business and cultural environment? How influential are they, and how detrimental might they be to the ongoing integration program?

> ## Misinformation

Have myths or rumors been created that are stalling cultural alignment? What is the "water cooler" talk? What negative, counter-productive misinformation needs to be addressed directly to effect unity and teamwork, forestall animosity, and avoid dips in productivity and morale?

> ## Reward and recognition

Such programs should have been immediately launched to support integration and the cultural alignment process. How are these programs being viewed? Do employees feel the programs are valuable, or do they feel they are a waste of time and not worthy of their involvement? (If so, the programs need to be speedily revamped – or scrapped and replaced with new ones.)

Sampling Strategies

Sampling involves selecting members from a given population in such a way that the input from those members is representative of the population as a whole. Sampling is necessary in large organizations. It allows a select number of employees to be surveyed – the theory holding that the sample will have the same characteristics and yield data in the same proportions as the total employee population.

Respondents identified through sampling must represent employee groups based on such variables as title (e.g., manager, supervisor, line worker, administrative); tenure (long-term employees versus those who joined the organization recently); and geography (in multi-office companies, employees from different parts of the country).

Employee samples should be drawn from both sides of the merged organization. There may be significant differences in how employees from the acquiring organization feel about merger-related issues in contrast to employees from the acquired firm. In multi-division firms, samples of employees might also need to be drawn from the different subsidiaries of the combined firm.

Assessment and Selection

*M*any mergers and acquisitions involve cost-reducing personnel cutbacks. Even transactions that do not involve layoffs invariably require realigning or re-deploying the employee base that results from combining two organizations. Clearly, a systematic approach to employee assessment and selection is needed after any sizable M&A transaction.

The determination must be made regarding the discrete skills and competencies necessary to support the merged company's growth initiatives. Thus, the strategic drivers of the merger will dictate the specific skills required to attain the sought-after synergies.

The most common strategic drivers, and the skills-related requirements of each, include:

➤ **Gaining new or complementary products**

Many times attaining new products requires retaining the developers and/or maintainers of those offerings. These professionals can include product managers, sales staff, customer-service representatives, and R&D and technical support personnel who work to bring the products to market and/or interface directly with customers.

➤ **Acquiring technology for manufacturing, product development or quality enhancement**

Staffing requirements and decision-making must ensure retaining the people who can understand, produce and market that technology (if it is product-driven) or who can utilize, maintain and upgrade technology (if it is production-driven).

➤ **Penetrate new markets or distribution channels**

If the M&A transaction is intended to penetrate a new geographic territory, it may be necessary to retain people with an intimate familiarity of that region and its customers. Often, geographic markets display distinct social, cultural and economic characteristics. These variables impact how goods and services are bought and sold. People familiar with those prevailing conditions are critical to succeeding in those markets.

➤ Acquiring production facilities

If the transaction is largely an asset deal (e.g., acquiring physical facilities as opposed to human capital) it may still be necessary to retain people who are familiar with the workings and maintenance of those facilities. This is particularly important if the facilities being purchased are intended to help the company realize manufacturing economies of scale and scope. Moreover, managers experienced in TQM (Total Quality Management) can make strong contributions to the merged firm's operations if they are transitioned quickly.

➤ Diversification

Diversification means that the merger or acquisition will take the acquirer into entirely new businesses or product areas. In such cases, it is necessary to keep in place all people from the acquired firm who are needed to manage the intricate workings of a business that may be significantly different from your own. Managers with technical expertise or familiarity with the local market environment should maintain their roles and leverage their knowledge deeper into the merged firm.

In sum: the goal of post-merger assessment and selection is identifying the people with the skills necessary to advance the new company's strategic initiatives. HR must take a *skills-based approach* to personnel decision-making.

By adopting this focus, HR spearheads the critical process of conducting personnel evaluations to determine which and how many employees must be retained to implement the combined company's growth strategies.

Behavioral and Workstyle Issues

Making post-merger personnel decisions based on strategic drivers provides the HR professional with an important frame of reference. However, making staff determinations also involves ensuring that an employee holds the competencies and behavioral traits necessary to succeed in a given role. This requires factoring in motivational and personality variables to determine if selected employees can function productively in the merged-company environment.

HR professionals must utilize state-of-the-art testing tools and techniques to support skills-based decision-making. These include tools that determine an employee's:

➢ **Abilities**

To measure his or her specific skills for a current position and for future roles in the organization

➢ **Workstyle**

To analyze individual traits that reveal the likelihood of a person succeeding in a given role

➢ **Behavioral traits**

To gauge his or her level of motivation and commitment, particularly in light of the person's attitudes toward the merged company and their current standing therein.

Taking a disciplined, empirical approach to post-merger personnel decision-making is essential. That is why HR professionals should avail themselves of the scientifically-based "psychometric" tools and testing techniques designed for use in assessment and selection. Ideally, these tools should be custom-designed to reflect the unique characteristics of the merged company and its organizational climate.

Training and Development

A specially designed curriculum of training and development courses is necessary to expedite post-merger integration. HR can also directly support management's growth initiatives by developing training that helps the merged firm attain the strategic drivers of the M&A transaction.

There are several basic categories that comprise the foundation of every post-merger training program. These include:

> **Benefits and retirement education**

   This is an area where employees pose the most questions in the wake of a merger or acquisition. They must be educated on the provisions of their new benefits plan, health insurance programs, and pension plans and defined-contribution retirement plans. Training is also required to instruct people on such tasks as completing and filing forms – as well as learning how to interface with internal benefits managers serving as informational contacts or advisors

> **Administrative procedures**

   In an acquisition, the target firm's employees must learn about how the acquiring company handles its day-to-day administrative activities. In situations where entirely new systems and procedures will be introduced (such as in a large-scale merger), all employees must learn new administrative practices such as completing purchase orders, filling out time sheets, submitting expense reports and making requisitions for office supplies.

> **Information technology**

   This is particularly important when merging or acquiring companies utilize proprietary technology applications that transcend conventional word-processing, spreadsheet, and other office management software. (Even a company that uses Microsoft Word™ must quickly train acquired employees if they come from a WordPerfect™ environment.) Training is critical to a speedy transition when the merged firm will be deploying new systems such as customer databases, computerized accounting systems, and programs for warehousing and tracking inventory.

➢ **Career development and counseling**

Employees must be educated on how their job performance will be evaluated, how this process differs from their previous assessment format, and how promotions and salary increases will be handled. It is often the case that combining companies have vastly dissimilar policies in the areas of employee evaluation and career pathing. These are areas of tremendous interest and sensitivity to employees — and must be addressed quickly in the training and development program schedule.

➢ **The corporate vision**

When everyone from the CEO on down understands the strategic goals of the transaction, and everyone has the same sense of strategic direction, then integration and cultural alignment can be effected. Espousing the corporate vision and the strategic tactics that will be used to realize it are key communication topics. Formalized training, however, is often a necessary supplement to employee communications to reinforce what is said in the printed word.

➢ **Merger partners' company history**

Employees must learn about their new partner's business beginnings and its current-day composition. This is necessary to engender empathy and respect for the organization and help foster unity and teamwork. (This topic could conceivably be covered in coursework on the corporate vision.)

➤ Product and service offerings

If every employee in the merged company is to truly become customer-focused, then training to describe the company's specific products and services is necessary. This topic should be covered in training for all levels of employees. It is especially critical — and should be more in-depth — for the combined company's sales and marketing and customer-contact personnel.

➤ Customer characteristics and requirements

Engendering a customer focus throughout the organization also requires that employees understand the customers being served by the merged company. All employees must be aware of who the firm's customers are, what needs those buyers have, and how the merged company will endeavor to meet those needs.

➤ Interpersonal and group communications

Interpersonal communication takes on tremendous importance in light of the challenges of integration and cultural alignment. In particular, verbal communication training is needed to ensure that new co-workers understand each other; it is especially crucial where there are significant language barriers (e.g., the combining companies use different terms or specific acronyms for business practices, units or processes). The channels of communication through which the combined company's employees will dialogue with each other must also be addressed — as should specific communication protocols that have or will be introduced.

In sum, employees must be trained in the customs, habits and history of the merger partners. An informed workforce is a stronger, more productive and more loyal one. Quickly sharing knowledge with your employees will boost morale and establish the bonds necessary to effect teamwork. An environment that demonstrates a commitment to training, development and career pathing will serve this mission.

Marketing and Sales

*E*ffecting corporate growth through revenue generation is the driving force of strategic mergers and acquisitions today. HR professionals must understand the revenue-focused strategies on which acquisition planning is now based. They must also recognize the role they play in directly supporting corporate growth initiatives.

"Marketing due diligence" was cited earlier. It is the process of identifying growth-related risks and opportunities in a given M&A transaction. A large part of marketing due diligence is identifying Revenue Enhancement Opportunities (REOs). An REO is a newly created or strengthened product or service that is forged by the fusion of two distinct attributes of merger partners and which generates immediate and/or long-term revenue growth. R.E.O.s typically take the form of:

1. Cross-selling opportunities

2. New products

3. Penetrating new markets or distribution channels

Although the design and execution of tactics to achieve REOs falls largely to sales and marketing managers, HR professionals contribute in critical ways. Following are examples of REOs, along with the activities HR would play in supporting revenue growth initiatives.

Case Study

Consider this example: A global insurance company and benefits consulting firm acquired a research firm that produces customized surveys for clients regarding the performance of their HMOs. Via marketing due diligence, several REOs were identified:

1. **Taking the target's HMO survey and creating a broadened consulting service offering.** The HMO survey could be the front-end of a consulting engagement that gauged employee usage patterns and likes and dislikes. The second phase of the engagement would involve consultants advising management on the current and future status of the HMO relationship, including revamping the terms and conducting subsequent negotiations with the health care provider.

2. **Cross-selling existing health and welfare consulting services to the target company's base of buyers of the HMO survey.** In this case, the acquirer had a strong and growing H&W consulting practice, and the target company had several hundred buyers of its HMO survey – companies with a demonstrated interest in H&W issues. The target's customers, therefore, represented viable prospects for the acquirer's H&W advisory services.

3. **Developing a new informational product – a research report – which could be marketed to clients and prospects of the merged firm and to the market at-large.** The REO resulted from the wealth of research data that the target firm had accumulated by conducting its HMO survey with companies of varying sizes, stages of growth and industry segments. The data could be summarized in a report developed for sale on an annual basis.

HR's role: REO initiatives of this nature would require HR's involvement in the following ways:

➢ T*raining* of the firm's H&W consultants to effectively understand and present the new products and services.

- If professional sales people needed to be hired, the *job specifications and skills sets would have to be identified*, and the *hiring process* coordinated by HR in concert with sales and marketing management.

- Any newly hired professionals would require swift indoctrination to the company and training on the specifics of the new products and the merged firm's complete range of offerings.

Strategically, HR must provide early and substantive input in identifying and planning REOs. This is because every REO has HR issues associated with it from a staffing and resource allocation standpoint. Remember: the financial impact of HR decisions relative to a given REO will directly impact both its conceptual viability and its ultimate profitability.

Specific REOs require specific support by HR. But as the earlier sections indicate, HR plays an even broader role in supporting post-merger growth initiatives in the areas of:

- **Managerial assessment and selection,** based on the skill sets required by the combined firm to advance its strategic initiatives

- **Training and development**, to expedite integration and effect longer-term cultural alignment

- **Organizational communications**, to unify, inspire and motivate employees – as well as engender a customer-focus throughout the company.

Conclusion

A multi-disciplinary understanding of mergers and acquisitions is needed if HR professionals are to successfully support their organizations' M&A activities.

HR professionals must broaden their functional frame of reference in order to evaluate the people-related ramifications of strategic and financial decisions made in M&A planning. Similarly, senior management must be more cognizant of critical HR issues that arise in acquisition decision-making. Experience shows that the latter has begun to occur. The survey findings indicate that respondents believe the former needs to occur as well.

There is no business event more challenging than orchestrating a merger or acquisition. HR's role is clearly moving from that of supporting cast member to star of the show. This increasingly pervasive trend points up the need for human resource professionals to be well-rehearsed when the M&A spotlight shines upon them.

NOTES